FROM A

TROUBLED

HOUSE

By Steve Cartwright

© Steve Cartwright 2019.

sccart@aol.com.

FROM A TROUBLED HOUSE

Used to chase perps, now I play with dogs

I used to rack a round into an APD-issued shotgun then move in behind the SWAT team as they kicked in a door and we searched for another armed perp and then I'd present my case against the perp before a jury and he was sent off to prison. Now I play with dogs. God is good!

Many memories, good and bad, started in my childhood house on DeLowe Dr. I no longer live in that troubled house, but *it* continues to live in me.

I've just discovered a new theater. It's in my mind and it's familiar because it's constructed of memories of a theater where I spent almost every Saturday afternoon of my youth. I am no longer young and my life has begun flashing before my eyes – that is why I find myself in this cinema deep in my subconscious.

I'm eating buttered popcorn, drinking a large Coke, because that's what I did as a kid in the theater. The price of admission is sleep.

Bits and pieces from my past started returning, and I wrote them down, in no particular order. When the big screen comes to life, it may be me as a frightened child fleeing in terror from my evil first stepmother. Or me as a cop as bullets seem to part my hair. Or it may be the first girl of whom I fell into that mystery known as love. Or it could be me and any of the thousands of dogs I Rescued.

I hear the projector as it turns on and the white, almost ice- blue, screen fills with light, and colorful images take form.....

The Growler, Jeeps in the mud

The Growler was a ritual that helped us climb a treacherous hill in the woods now part of the Camp Creek Parkway development.

Me and friends drove Jeep CJ7s and Toyota Land Cruisers.

The Hill involved in The Growler ritual was always rocky and muddy, and once you start up it, the terrain tried to rip your fists from the steering wheel and chunk your Jeep down a jagged ravine.

At the base of The Hill, our adrenaline pounding like war drums, I'd engage the hill and we'd all take a burning slug of The Growler -- MD 2020, cheap wine with the bouquet of kerosene. We'd whoop and holler, and at the summit, the smell of mud sizzling on the hot engine, we'd pop open cold Miller Lites and shoot guns for hours.

Mrs Wright

One day after the mandatory nuclear blast drill, my Conley Hills 7th grade teacher, Mrs Beverley Wright, sat maternally in a rocker and told us to sit around her.

She read from a book in her lap, "Huck Finn" by Mark Twain, and this East Point fat boy was electrified. As I would grow more sophisticated, I would realize my literary hero was great at lampooning fatcat fortune-hunters while being the biggest fortune-hunter alive.

One rainy morn, Mrs Wright dropped the needle on a phono and, from the internal speaker, accompanied by pops and hisses, I was in rapture listening to "Triumphal March from Aida" and Strauss' magnificent "Waltz of the Blue Danube". Not only did Mrs Wright turn me on to classical music, she, a fellow artist, helped me develop my drawing ability.

I've called her several times to tell her that many of her interests resonated with me. But she was out every time I called. I'm glad she's staying busy in retirement, but I'd love for her to know she was my most influential Conley Hills teacher.

Use Tow Truck To Yank Off Felon's Burglar Door

"Our perp is telling all his thug buddies he won't be taken alive," said the detective with the arrest warrant, lighting a cigarette with a flame illuminating his face in the summer night.

We stood next to a city-contract tow truck, the drum clanking as the wrecker driver manually unraveled the cable and piled it in the back as we cops, detectives and uniformed SWAT officers, discussed how we planned to arrest a violent felon.

"My snitch says my perp just snuck into his girlfriend's house," the lead detective continued, blowing smoke, "so if we move FAST we'll literally catch him with his pants down."

We had clandestinely surveiled the house and every door and window had metal burglar bars. And we had to get in and capture the perp before he could reach his weapons and make good on his bragging.

"That's fifty feet of cable," said the wrecker driver, stopping the winch and lighting a Winston with trembling fingers.

"Let's hit it then," said the lead detective, grinding his cigarette out in the street where zone cops had stopped all traffic.

SWAT cops, invisible in the night in their black tactical garb, ran to cover the back and sides of the tiny house we had parked two blocks away from. The wrecker driver stopped, hovered his cowboy boot above the accelerator, and puffed smoke in his cab. The lead detective grabbed the hook from the truck and sprinted to the front door and secured it to the metal door, signaled the driver who screeched forward, yanking the burglar door from the wall and flinging it thirty feet. SWAT cops with entrance tools demolished the wooden door and the team rushed in. The perp was naked in bed with his girlfriend; he started to grab his gun on the floor, then changed his mind about not being taken alive, and quickly raised his hands.

Gigi Helps Troubled Girl

The tablecloth jerked, being yanked off, knocking over our Rescue tips jar – but no one was there!

Then I saw a bit of cloth had dipped into Gigi's crate and she was tugging it with all her pittie strength.

"No, Gigi!" commanded Rescue Lady Diane, snatching it from one of our favorite Rescue's jaws. "She's getting Shelter Syndrome, I swear," she muttered to me, looking at the ripped cloth in her hands. "She's started tearing her bedding at the shelter; she didn't use to do that!" Gigi was reacting to living in a cage when all she wanted was a loving home with her own bed. Eventually she was adopted by Sally and the bad habits vanished like that tablecloth did. Sally couldn't stand being separated from Gi (renamed "Ruby") so, cautiously, brought her to where she worked as a therapist. Soon many of Sally's patients greeted Ruby in her bed before they said hi to their shrink.

One afternoon a troubled teen sat rigidly on the patient couch, eyes lowered, hands clasped firmly, her dark hair matted from compulsive twirling. Ruby's head jerked up; she crossed to the troubled girl and laid her head gently in her lap. This girl had never done more than mumble in her previous sessions, but now she laughed, hugged Ruby, and spoke. Love heals – dogs as well as people.

At One Point, You Played With Friends The Last Time

Maybe me and my friends played HORSE at the basketball goal we all had in our East Point back yards. Maybe we could hear a thunderstorm approaching, ominously. At one point, all of us played with our friends, not knowing it would be the last time. We would have separated and run home alone, the door slamming behind us, cutting you off as your path merged away from theirs.

Feel I Could Walk Out My Door To EP Past

Sometimes I feel like I could swing open my front door and walk out in East Point and have clam chowder at Captain's Roost. Or be at a pep rally while the HHS marching band plays music so loud the entire gym, and my bones, are vibrating.

Or all the friend chicken and roast beef I, a fat boy, could eat at the Smorgasbord. Or playing Putt Putt on a hot summer night while swilling Mountain Dew in a paper cup with a prize printed on the bottom.

Or sitting at Gigi's as the waitress brings me pizza with the cheese still bubbling. Or sitting in the Greenbriar theater balcony with a tub of buttered popcorn and large Coke. Or at Wingo's dipping a bite of KC steak into their mysterious, black sauce.

Or in Conley Hills as my 7th grade teacher introduces the class to classical music via scratchy records on a battered phono.

Shows I watched on Star Trek were full of space ships going faster than the speed of light and sending them back in time. I guess my front door just doesn't open that fast!

Dog Rescue good vs evil

I thought when I retired from APD the battle of good vs evil was like my blue uniform hanging, hidden, in the closet.

But yesterday I saw the newest pup rescued from the shelter, a little guy named Chance, his black fur bearing the scars of where a human monster threw him, a bait dog, into a pit with fighting dogs, and I am reminded of The Who song lyrics: "I'm a soldier at 63!"

Tail tucked, his brown eyes scrutinize me to see if I treat him the way humans have previously treated him. Letting him sniff my hand, I like to think there's a spiritual aspect to Rescue, that God sends me where I can do good.

Chance timidly wags, once, then tucks again. I offer a treat. He sniffs it, looks into my eyes again; timidly he takes and chews as if expecting I'm going to snatch it away from him. Tail twitches again, wanting me to be a friend.

I specialize in working with the abused Rescues who are scared. I've developed what I call The First Law of Dog Rescue; every dog in the so-called shelter has been abused some how, and it is imperative that the Rescuer uses love to undo the evil done to them.

Chance needed a friend. He allowed me to hug him. "I am your friend, Chance." The start of a slow process; a battle in a never-ending war.

Cass, Christy, Mango – my pack

As a white pup, Cassie was kept chained to a tree in all weather; now she has the run of my house and back yard.

Christy was beaten so bad, then penned in the PTC Petco dumpster, we feared she'd lose an eye; now she wants to stay so close to me that she often sleeps on my chest.

Mango was terrified of all people; now she sits next to me while I'm on the computer, and watches me with a look of sweet love.

Now they are my pack and they run together in my yard, chasing tomato-eating chipmunks, and we sleep as tightly together as a jigsaw puzzle.

All Us Boys Had Tree Huts

All us boys had tree huts. Even if all it was was a plank laid as evenly as possible between two strong branches so we could sit on it and dangle our feet. If an "enemy" should walk underneath, we'd drop a pinecone on their head and *laugh*.

One father, no doubt reliving his own long-past boyhood, built his son a tree *mansion*. When it was done we gathered to marvel at it. Unlike our jobs, it was proportional, made mostly of plywood bearing pencil marks as guides for where his dad put nails and doors and windows.

What really took our breath away was a skylight made of clear plastic.

Climb Tree To See Equitable Tower

The 32-stories-tall Equitable Building joined Atlanta's skyline in 1968 when I was 12.

In East Point, I had a neighbor who had a tall tree on a hill in their back yard. One Saturday afternoon I climbed that tree, as all us kids did, but something made me go higher, and higher still, than any of us had done before.

When I climbed as far as I could, I looked around from my exalted height. I could see the Atlanta skyline, and Equitable was prominent. I felt a stirring in my adolescent body, hugging that rough bark where only birds dwell. We kids mispronounced the skyscraper's name as "E-quit-able"

Survivor's Guilt

His cigarette, forgotten, has left a long ash at the edge of the wooden table in the corner of smoky, crowded Manuel's Tavern. It was 1979 and I was a rookie, thankful to be invited to join some APD veterans unwinding after a summer-hot, bloody, busy evening watch.

As cold, amber pitchers of beer were poured; as war stories, old and some just lived, were being told, I noticed one of the cops splayed his hand on the table and started jabbing between his fingers with a switch-blade knife. He was older than me so protocol wouldn't allow me to interrupt his odd game.

As the knife made clunking noises into the table, I recalled he had been a Marine in Vietnam and almost everyone in his squad had been killed in one firefight. I'd taken enough college psych classes to recognize survivor's guilt, a mental condition that occurs when a person believes they have done something wrong by surviving a traumatic event when others did not. As if he'd read my mind, he turned his boyish, Irish face toward me, expressionless, then removed his hand from the table and, making a fist, studied the old scars there.

I knew he wasn't going to speak to me; I was just a rookie and he was a veteran, and older than me.

My Life Seems To Be Passing Before My Eyes Like Those Black-and-white Newsreels

My life seems to be passing before my eyes like those black-and-white Newsreels that used to play in theaters before the Pink Panther cartoon. Memories are just coded chemicals along countless neurons in our brain like villages along a windless river: classroom snippets from Headland HS; childhood memories of playing ball on a summer day at Grayson field; my first day as a reporter at the *Atlanta Suburban Reporter*; my last day walking away from APD.

Newsreels grow brittle and sometimes break, the celluloid slapping round and round as the projectionist sprints up the stairs from the restroom.

Attacked By Our Pet Geese

The attack on me was quick, loud, and brutal. I was a chubby 8-year-old in 1964 but Beauregard was one big, mean goose!

When we lived on DeLowe Dr, one of my evil stepsisters wanted two baby geese for Easter, and if she wanted something, she got it. The little white geese were so cute and made cooing sounds, but they quickly grew to some 30 pounds and lived in our fenced-in backyard.

Beauregard, and his smaller sister Hildegarde, seeing me enter their domain, would honk and bite me. One hot day after school, they got me good;

Beauregard rushed me, honking like the horns around Jericho, and grabbed my blue jeans at the knee where I couldn't escape, and he spread his huge wings and swung them, like a Kung Fu master, clipping me behind my knee and sending me sprawling into the summer grass, them biting me.

In desperation, I punched their heads, which made them swivel on their long necks. Fighting to stand, I grabbed rocks and pelted the foul fowls, forcing their honking retreat. Hildegarde screamed when a rock hit her and I panicked when I saw blood dripping from her orange beak.

In tears, fearing I killed her, I snatched paper towels from the kitchen and held her in my lap, wiping away her blood. I would later learn that fighting back against a bully often transformed them into your friend, and that happened with her.

My father gave the brute Beauregard to a relative in the country and we kept Hildegarde, who became a loving pet to me. One winter morning I found her dead body behind a bush and I cried inconsolably for her.

I couldn't, but some sensitive people can feel its presence. The angel of death perched in a tree in our yard, casting a shadow darker than night.

Towns and Buildings At Lake Lanier Bottom

All my life I've been fascinated by lore about what lies at the bottom of Lake Lanier.

When the dam was built and water flowed in, whole towns became flooded, covering roofs and church steeples and rising higher than the Statue of Liberty at some spots.

I heard strange Lake Lanier legends at recess at Conley Hills Elementary, at YMCA and Boy Scout camps.

One story was about a kid (our horror stories were usually about fellow kids) who jumped into the lake and surfaced screaming, onlookers startled to see his head wrapped with snakes, biting him!

My imagination saw trucks frozen in slimy water on submerged town squares where community bells sway in the swift currents, with muted clangings sending up bubbles. Tales of catfish the size of Volkswagons titillated my imagination, as did campfire stories of teen swimmers drowning after something grabbed their ankle; divers seeking the body reported the drowning took place above a flooded graveyard....

Selective Service Board

I sat goofing off in my 11th grade desk, when a student-aide handed me a mysterious hall pass and told me I was wanted in the cafeteria.

Once there, a male teacher said "Take a seat!", pointing to a metal folding chair, which I slouched into, a teen with poor posture. I faced a cafeteria table, behind which sat three men, each writing with a pen onto a stack of papers.

"Name," said the older man in the middle, not looking up. With wiseacre voice, I answered; then was asked my age, address, and plans beyond high school. Suddenly the outside world rushed in like floodwater. Every night on the news with Walter Cronkite the Vietnam War was being fought. This, I realized, sitting up straight, was The Draft Board. Not in a federal building with long steps and marble columns, but in my own school cafeteria. I could smell lunch starting to cook, and nervously cleared my throat, wondering what to do with my suddenly trembling hands.

My Mother Waves Bye From Hospital Window

On That Day in 1960 my father easily hoisted me onto his big shoulders and pointed up to the window on the third floor of Crawford Long Hospital. (East Point would not get South Fulton Hospital for another three years.)

I saw a nurse helping my mother to the window up above. I have diagnosed myself with OCD, after only a few college psych courses. Every time I leave home, the OCD predicts a fire. Driving, it warns that a Mack truck *could* bust a red light and T-bone me. Any one or thing I love, OCD sees only pending death.

"Wave goodbye to your mommy," my father said, his voice cracking, and I dutifully waved up as she waved to me, from a distance that would only grow larger. Three days later the OCD would start, and never stop.

Pilled-out Babysitter Passes Out Into Her Strawberry Shortcake While I Watch

My mother died when I was 4 and my father hired a woman, a stranger, to babysit me while he and my 18-year-old brother Jody were at work.

She was a drug-abuser; that's probably why she wore sunglasses in our DeLowe Dr house.

One afternoon she laid strawberry shortcake on the kitchen table and passed out face-first into the dessert. Climbing on the table, I lifted up her face, covered in whipped cream, and asked her what she was doing.

No answer, so I dropped her head back into the bowl and waddled to play in the near-by creek. Jody came home for lunch and the babysitter was still in the shortcake and I did not answer his calls. The next day, an aunt took over babysitting me.

Alvin and Chipmunks Sing Beatles' Songs album

When I was a child, my father would not allow me to have any Beatles songs, and he controlled the money. I thought I was clever when I got him to buy me the album of Alvin and the Chipmunks singing Beatles songs. I figgered they just sped up Beatles recordings to make it sound like Alvin and the gang singing, so I'd just slow my cheap record player to a lower speed and -- *voila!* Didn't work. Of course. And that's how I came to own an Alvin and the Chipmunks album.

Bev Was My Friend

She stumbled through our Ben Hill Rd neighborhood looking like an emaciated witch, wearing the same clothes for months. I was retired at the time.

A Good Samaritan decided she'd deliver some food to Beverley's neglected house, and asked me to tag along. Beverley opened the door, the smell of rot and stale cigarette smoke rolled out with her, and she sneered at the food, slurring: "I wouldn't eat this crap! But, if you got me a Varsity hot dog..."

I didn't want to waste my time on an old drunk, but over the weeks we had many astounding conversations and, when she wasn't too drunk, she was surprisingly articulate and perceptive.

When she moved to an Assisted Living facility, I visited her every Saturday, and we spoke daily on the phone. To my amazement, I learned she was once a scientist at Ga Tech and every day she and the other scientists walked to the Varsity for lunch. Beverley married an Air Force pilot and became pregnant. Cigarette smoke obscured some of her face as she paused, eyes tearing. A plane crash left her a pregnant widow and, I realized, left her drowning in the bottle.

In Assisted Living, a kind staff member kept her clothes clean and Bev enjoyed playing group trivia, and holding the house cat. Turns out she really loved cats, but hadn't had a pet in decades.

The nice employee called one day: "Bev fell out and was transported to Piedmont." I planned to visit Bev, share Varsity hot dogs and gift her a cat-calender. But federal law would not let Piedmont divulge if Bev was even a patient, and she died after three days. Her East Point house, a hoarder's dream where roaches ambled unafraid, is falling in on itself, the same way Bev's life did when that Air Force jet crashed and burned. Bev was my friend.

At one point Bev was put into an Alzheimer facility; she had problems but she was not crazy. She quickly learned the code to the door and came and went as she pleased. We eventually got her moved into Assisted Living. She was very proud of breaking that code!

East Point "Witch" Collected Clovers From Kids

When I was a kid on DeLowe Dr me and my friends lived in houses. But our parents' houses were surrounded by woods. Deep, dark, mysterious woods.

There was a "witch's" house on Mulberry Ct we had to pass to enter that secluded fantasyland. An old lady with white hair lived alone in the shadowy house. She'd pay us a penny if we brought her a clover. "I *love* 4-leaf clovers," she'd tell us. "Those are good luck. But I'll pay you sweet children a penny for *any* clover you bring me." It was like a toll we paid to cross her lawn and enter the woods.

Maybe, we laughed among ourselves, she's a witch, and she threw the clovers into a bubbling cauldron, concocting her witch's brew. We kids grabbed clovers from her yard and ran back to her door to collect our pennies.

Free of the witch, we sprinted into the woods to play War, or Dragons and Knights.

Looking back now, all these decades – maybe she wasn't a witch after all, but a lonely old woman playing a gentle game to entice us into her silent kitchen.

After a morning of play, we'd head home for a nap, and pass back by the "witch's" shadowy house. I often saw her, still at her window, watching us kids and waving, sadly, as we rushed home, crushing all those clovers as we ran, laughing, over her lawn.

Phonetic Madness My Dad Wanted Me To Sing In Church Choir

When I was a kid my father wanted me to sing in our church choir. Not that he had anything against our church, East Point First Methodist, just that they went on a multi-state tour of churches to sing and he thought that would be good for me.

Trouble was, I was tone deaf; I can look at a musical note and it is unfathomable how I could translate that into a dulcet tone coming out of my chubby throat. But he insisted. The entire tour I lip-synched. Had I have actually sung, the bus driver would have pushed us all back onto the bus and sped back to East Point, not even stopping for toll booths. Such is the nature of phonetically induced madness.

Altzheimer Patient Enters Lassiter's POV

We'd just left the Zone 2 precinct, now I was whipping our unmarked APD car around and speeding back there.

Unit 206 radioed my partner: "Is there supposed to be someone in your POV?" [personally-owned vehicle] That's when I turned us back around and my partner threw the blue light globe onto the dashboard.

"Negative!" he radioed back, gripping his metal flashlight like a club. We were zipping around cars on Ponce de Leon NE, in 1979 when the Zone 2 precinct was across from the monolithic Sears building.

I could see his pickup truck up ahead and I yanked the Velcro strap from the S and W .38 in my shoulder holster.

Skidding to a stop, we leapt out of the car, but hesitated when we saw an old man behind the wheel of Gene's pickup, the door open.

"What are you doing in my truck!" Gene exclaimed and I could see the man was confused. And frightened. "I want to drive home," he said, his age-spotted hands trembling as they moved over the dashboard like it was red-hot.

Knowing there was an old folks' home nearby, I radioed for our dispatcher to call there and ask if they were missing a resident.

"They are," the dispatcher responded. "He has dementia."

I re-snapped my revolver. "We're familiar," I radioed back. Within minutes a rotund nurse joined us and called the gentleman's name: "Come on, Chester. Let's go home."

"That's where I'm trying to go," he cried, looking around this unfamiliar world he found himself in. He compliantly went with the nurse, though she must have seemed a stranger to him.

As a kid I believed the Outer Limits Control Voice

As a little kid I was the official TV set-adjuster in our family. For the longest time I believed the Outer Limits Control Voice when he said they were in control of our television. I don't recall any rolling or other problems during their show!

Abused Skipper Lap Therapy

When I was told our new Rescue Skipper lived almost all of his two years of life chained to a tree, I knew I had to sit in the pen with him to assess him.

Nervous at first, we quickly became buddies and he sat in my lap and kissed me like abused dogs often do; I call this Lap Therapy.

His foster had only agreed to help transport him on a leg of his trip to New York, but when the other transports fell through, she reluctantly took Skipper home. And fell in love with him, just like I did at today's adoption. Just like other folks did, including a customer who wanted to be a volunteer just to spend more time with this sweetie.

Chase Perp Into MARTA Construction Tunnel

I was a Zone 2 Field Investigator when I made my descent into the underworld.

The MARTA underground line was being dug that summer. This evening was hot summer and I wore a black tee shirt with my jeans.

I spotted a felon I had a warrant for, strolling down Peachtree Street, and as soon as he saw my unmarked detective car heading his way, he put it in the wind.

"Unit 222 in pursuit of a felony suspect!" I radioed as my adrenaline kicked in to high gear. He ran through where they were constructing the MARTA Midtown station and I had to jump out after him.

He ran into the huge hole, lit sparingly with flood lights, and as we descended into the earth, I could no longer hear the sirens of my approaching backup units, nor would my police radio transmit or receive.

I slipped and slid in the mud, as no concrete had yet been poured there, and the air turned frigid at that low level and I could see my breaths. I was tired, but the perp was more tired, and I caught and cuffed him.

Back on the surface of the world, it was torrid hot and the Midtown night pulsed with a dozen flashing blue lights.

Here I introduce you to my wicked first stepmother, who troubled my childhood house.

Evil Stepmom Installs AC, Excludes Me

Our house in East Point suddenly had two temperature zones in the summer of 1963: sweat-inducing heat and heavenly cool.

My evil stepmother's parents, well-to-do Douglas County ranch-owners, installed central AC and gave us their old window unit. It could have cooled our entire house, but, then, my Step wouldn't be tormenting me, so it went in the parental bedroom and a hall door was kept closed so her two equally-evil daughters could share in the oasis. The rest of the abode, including my room on the opposite end, remained oppressive for me and my best friend, a Boston terrier named Judy. When the heat got too much, I'd clandestinely open that forbidden hall door and step into another, cool, cool world. Until I was caught and again kicked out of paradise.

Ain't Love Grand? Well, Ain't It?

Cindy was my first girlfriend.

We were both around 9 and she lived a block away. She sent her younger brother, Steven, to tell me she wanted to be my girlfriend. I didn't know what to say. If she was willing to overlook me being chubby, I was willing to overlook her being slightly cross-eyed.

But I was shy, and within the hour Steven returned to tell me Cindy decided to break up with me.

I was devastated and found myself driving my red bike round and round her block, hoping she'd notice me.

I hardly dated as a teen because I had no self-confidence, still being chubby and having terrible acne.

Self-confidence came after being hired as a cop, and I made up for lost time. I dated plenty of hot strippers because the Cheetah 3 was on my beat and I frequented the place, "practicing my powers of observation".

The strippers were sexy, they liked to take off their clothes, but most were freaky. Not the kind of girl you bring home to meet mother, especially if you don't have a mother.

The other women I dated stayed with me longer, and that brought back the pain from childhood: my mother dying, the evil stepmother and her daughters invading our house. Life in that house on DeLowe Dr has troubled me for the rest of my life.

Rodney King Atl riots

The Rodney King riots in downtown Atlanta: Sopping up after the worst of the riot was over, I gazed at all the bricks and rocks littering the dead Downtown streets and sidewalks.

It seemed that every glass storefront on Peachtree Street was shattered. Voices over the radio strapped to my gunbelt were calling about burglaries here and there. Under protection of the anarchy of the angry crowds, burglars and looters had gone wild. Now we were retaking Downtown, and I couldn't remember how long I'd gone without food or drink.

As I ducked through yet another shattered store window, illuminating its ruined innards with my flashlight, I mused about chaos. Is order something most humans seek, disdaining bedlam?

The city was now calm, yet in the back of this dark store I heard the sound of people running. We caught three burglars hiding behind spilled racks of clothing. Gun drawn, I yelled: "On the floor! On the floor!"

After handcuffing them, we led them back out to the street and loaded them into an already overstuffed paddy wagon.

Taking a quick smoke break, me and two other cops were silent. Looking at all the rocks and bricks, I thought how much Downtown looked like the surface of the moon.

During a lull in the fighting, a GSP truck, bearing hundreds of donated Chick-filas, scooted to our location. I wolfed down two in a matter of seconds, with no drink to wash them down with.

Judy

There was no hugging or kissing or "I love you"'s in my childhood house. Except from Judy.

I smile thinking about how she'd put her front paws on top of the stool fan so it could cool her belly.

My first stepmother ordered my father to put in a window AC to cool everyone else's rooms but mine. My step-family was like an invading army; for the hatred radiated on me by Sara, she loved and praised her two teen daughters.

But I had Judy – to hug, to kiss, to love, and laugh at the black and white Boston Terrier's antics. She lived into the era of my second stepmother and died in my lap. Not the last dog to break my heart in this life.

Dog Rescue Good vs Evil

I thought when I retired from APD the battle of good vs. evil was like my blue uniform hanging, hidden, in the closet.

But yesterday I saw the newest pup rescued from the shelter, a little guy named Chance, his black fur bearing the scars of where a human monster threw him, a bait dog, into a pit with fighting dogs, and I am reminded of The Who song lyrics: "I'm a soldier at 63!"

Tail tucked, brown eyes scrutinizing me to see if I treat him the way humans have previously treated him. Letting him sniff my hand, I like to think there's a spiritual aspect to Rescue, that God sends me where I can do good.

Chance timidly wags, once, then tucks again. I offer a treat. He sniffs it, looks into my eyes again; timidly he takes and chews as if expecting I'm going to snatch it away from him. Tail twitches again, wanting me to be a friend. Chance needs a friend. He allows me to hug him.

"I am your friend, Chance." The start of a slow process; a battle in a never-ending war.

Carnival

It was torture! Gazing out the classroom window into the playground below where parent-volunteers were constructing the Conley Hills Elementary Halloween Carnival.

I only averted my eyes to check the big, round clock hanging above the blackboard. The teacher finally gave up trying to teach, and released us early. Hundreds of running Keds carried us to the promised land!

I bought cotton candy and, as I ate the sweet cloud-like treat, some stuck to my eyebrows, giving me old-man brows. At a table, used books sold for a few pennies; I bought two James Bond novels and James Michener's huge "Hawaii". The chill October night came quickly and lights came on, casting shadows in the lot I'd only known in daylight. A classmate's father was grilling hotdogs and hamburgers, and I kept him busy. In a tent marked HAUNTED HOUSE, a gypsy said the spirits told her I had a dog named Judy, but I recognized my neighbor beneath the heavy make-up. In a classroom, instead of a boring social studies film, I paid a dime to laugh at "Abbott and Costello Go to Mars" while munching popcorn.

I eventually had to go home; but, in a way, I never really left that place.

News Daily Staff Eat Lunch Together

Our South Fulton *News-Daily* staff enjoyed lunches laughing together.

As an 18 year-old staff Reporter / cartoonist, and only East Point resident, I often guided my fellow journalists to eating places such as: Johnny Reb's in College Park; I still recall the fried chicken, huge glasses of sweet tea, and wooden cane-bottom chairs. Joyful Noise and their heavenly roast beef and gravy. Captain's Roost and the first clam chowder my unsophisticated taste buds ever savored. BBQ Kitchen and their free veggie re-orders. Flying Pig, a BBQ joint behind a liquor store; we'd wolf down these sandwiches at our desks while we typed on our Underwoods, racing to beat our deadlines. Kountry Kitchen -- hamburger steak baptized with Heinz 57, and french fries hot enough to burn your mouth.

Our staff used to challenge our rivals, the SF Neighbor staff, to pizza-eating contests at the Pizza Hut buffet on Virginia Ave at the airport -- they sure were sore losers! Tasteful journalism!

I Wear Shorts In Winter To Understand Pets Chained Outside

I wear shorts and tee-shirts most of the year. When it's painfully cold, I use that to experience a little of what pets go through chained outside. Of course, I don't live outside. I can scurry inside where my bed is warm and so is my food. And I wish I could bring all the cowering dogs inside with me. We'd have a great time together. We'd play, then eat so much we fall asleep cuddling and dreaming happily. Safe. Dry. Warm.

My First Home-made Cinnamon Roll

I was in my bedroom on DeLowe Dr, drawing with a pencil on blue-lined paper I was supposed to be doing my Conley Hills homework on, when my 8-year-old nostrils detected the loveliest smell they'd ever smelt.

The pencil dropped from my chubby fingers and I followed the aroma into the kitchen. My stepsister, already a teen, was using a spoon to ladle a white topping onto Pillsbury Cinnamon Rolls in a hot pan. I salivated watching that icing melt and run like tempting lava down those brown rolls.

"Let's see if Steven likes them," one step said to her older sis as they stood at the hot stove like witches cackling over a bubbling cauldron. "Since this is our first time baking these."

Without a word toward me (they considered me as lowly as the house dog, a stranger in my own house ever since my father married their loathsome mother), she scooped one cinnamon roll onto a napkin and handed it to me. It burned my mouth, but I'd learned in church pleasure must come with sacrifice. The icing merged with the doughy roll and I was in ecstasy. I ate every cinnamon roll in the pan and looked for more.

"I'd say they are a success!" one step said to the other and they returned to their bedroom, slamming the door.

I returned to my own room in a sugar high and looked at my pencil resting on the paper tablet. How like a cinnamon roll that brown pencil looked!

Greenbriar and Westgate Theaters

As a kid I would leave the world of light to bask in the world of darkness, armed only with a tub of buttered popcorn and large Coke. A quarter got me into the Westgate or Greenbriar theater, a mysterious world of the inner mind. A Pink Panther cartoon, previews, then movies I loved like the James Bond films, Dean Martin as superspy Matt Helm -- 2001: A Space Odyssey!

But when they ended, I was back in the harsh world again, having to shield my eyes from the painful light.

Descending into the dark netherworld of dreams, the smell of popping corn was like the Siren's song to the olfactory. A kid's matinee ticket at the Greenbriar theater was 75 cents. Large buttered popcorn & a large Coke were another 75 cents. Even the restroom was shadowed, like a Stanley Kubrick set; the Muzak softly whispering as though its tower were on Mars. The theater was dark, so the dreamer could dream. Later, riding the escalator back up into the world of light, hurting my eyes, I, like all other kids, stomped my tennis shoes to make those strange, Greenbriarian echoes.

My Fascination of A House Being Built

A house was being built near ours in East Point; the sound of hammers pounding, the heavy smell of sawdust in the summer sun.

I was six and mesmerized watching them build it day by day, a pile turning into a finished house. My mother had become sick, and died, and my father, emotionally unable to raise a mother-less child, had a plan: like in a torrynado, as I called them, I was often shuttled off to visit so many family and friends that I always awoke and had to look around to realize where I was that day.

I watched the builders construct a concrete foundation, straight and strong; next came a tall skeleton of pleasant-smelling planks, and then the walls, and a roof spreading like protective arms. I knew in my head, not even a big ole torrynado could tear that house down! I'm still fascinated watching a house being built.

Rescue Jack Is One of My Favorite Success Stories

When I first assessed him all he did was try to flee me, panicked. When I last saw him, he kissed me goodbye before leaving with his new family.

In my many years in dog Rescue, I consider the transformation of Jack as one of my greatest memories.

NCHS rescued him as he lay dying in the shelter; some monster had starved him almost to death and there was evidence suggesting he'd been used as target practice with a pellet gun. The owners of Puppy Tubs, Tom and Laurie Clarke, rescue dog angels, allowed us to house 3 of our dogs there for free. When Laurie first laid her kind eyes on the weak, dying English black lab, she burst into tears and took Jack on as her special project, nursing him back to health.

Part of my mission for God is to try to undo the evil done to abused Rescues, but I feared Jack was beyond any earthly help. I spent hours with him in a room, just talking calmly to him; but when I introduced him to Wrangler, another Rescue, and Jack saw how a happy dog played with someone who loves them, he slowly began getting better. Nine months with a foster with 2 other dogs let Jack learn the joy of sleeping in a bed and playing with his own toys.

So, when Jack got adopted, my voice cracked as I tearfully told my sweet friend goodbye and wished him the happy life he deserves!

Sara Attacks Me in My Sandbox

I stared, for what seemed like hours, at the divot in my sandbox. I was probably 9 and I knew something significant had just happened here.

It wasn't the first time Sara, my first stepmother, had physically attacked me. Not long before this, I'd been playing at my friend David's house. Sara phoned and told David's mom I needed to come home immediately. I did, only to find Sara hiding behind our front door. In a mad frenzy she started beating my legs with a strip of wood moulding. Screaming hysterically, I ran to my bedroom and locked myself inside, cradling my dog Judy, not knowing what Sara would do next. She went outside to her car and drove to Greenbriar mall and went shopping.

So when I was playing with plastic soldiers in my sandbox and looked up and saw Sara, big as an alligator-fightin' woman, rushing toward me with a look of hate, I knew I had to escape.

Trying to snatch me, she grabbed my shirt and I spun around, everything slowing, and how well I recall looking up at her big belly, and without thinking, I pushed with both hands into her gut. She fell backward into the white sand and looked at me in surprise. "I'll get you for this!" she hissed, standing up and brushing sand from her blue skirt. She glared at me as she returned to the house.

I lived in fear of her "getting me back" but she never hit me again. Ever. I learned a lesson that morning about bullies.

I sat and stared at that divot in my white sand box, that Grand Canyon, for hours and hours and hours.

Dad Saves A Toddler

Dad saw the car rolling, occupied only by a toddler hanging happily in the open window.

Slamming our car into Park, he leaped out, ran to the other car slowly rolling down the slight incline of the Harris Jr convenience store, jumped in and stopped the runaway car, the kid slobbering on the shoulder of Dad's postal uniform shirt.

As he returned to properly park our car, a woman exited the glass door, clutching a little brown bag, smiled at Dad and called a polite "Thanks", and then boredly drove away.

This insensed me, then 10 years old. "*Thanks?!* You just saved her kid and her car from rolling into DeLowe Dr traffic! She doesn't even shake your hand?!"

Dad smiled modestly and shrugged. I knew he did the Christian thing without expecting praise...but, *still!*

Inside Harris Jr, he paid a dime for that day's *Atlanta Journal* and I got a cherry Coke Slurpee and Sugar Babies, unable to fathom some – most – all – adults.

Chased by a ghost as a kid?

When I was a kid in 1960, I was convinced I'd been chased by a ghost.

My mother died when I was 4, living in East Point, and I got shuffled around to stay with relatives. An old granny house can be very frightening, especially to a kid who just lost his mother. My paternal grandmother lived on Melrose Dr in southwest Atlanta. I explored her house and opened a door and saw wooden stairs descending down to the very core of the earth.

I was ordered into a back bedroom for naps. The bed was next to a window and the yellowed blinds, I thought, were made of human skin.

But the scariest house they sent me to was my maternal grandmother's on Lexington Ave SW. My grandfather died before he could complete the basement; the foundation planks were in place without a floor, so I could walk along, like on a high wire, and see the shadowed, muddy ground. No doubt snakes were there, waiting for me to fall through.

The back porch was on high stilts that swayed when you walked on its floor.

They had a painting illuminated by an interior bulb that gave it a ghostly appearance in the living room.

Light bulbs hung from the stippled ceiling on cords, like snakes, and, at night, caused murky pools of light in the spooky darkness. When my grandmother and me were watching TV in the living room, where the ghostly painting hung, and she told me to run off to bed, it was through that darkness I had to run. Crying with fear, I entered the hallway where I saw what had to be a ghost! I ran back to the light and hid my head in my grandmother's lap.

So, when I was a teenager and I had to return to that house with my father after my grandmother died, I again saw the ghost in the hall who had chased me. It was a full-length mirror. My, my, how that ghost had grown!

Cannon I Played On Seemed Huge

When Dad went inside the East Point city hall, I loved playing on the cannon in the front lawn. At the time it seemed huge enough to make craters on the moon.

Now I know it's not a cannon, but a howitzer. I'd straddle the barrel and scoot, scoot, scoot seemingly high into the sky, where I'd lean over and stare into the dark bore and scream into it expecting to hear echoes.

Looking at a photo of my cannon, I am shocked at how small it really is.

Remembering My Childhood Church

Although I still live in East Point, I attend church in Fayetteville, as do several escapees from current day East Point. My pastor's tribute to my father, in a 2018 sermon, as his Sunday School teacher in our youth, triggered memories of that old

East Point church; me electrified by mighty hymns such as "Amazing Grace"; a preacher's stage whisper rolling into speaker-shaking exultations; fearfully hearing how Abraham tied his son Issac to the altar, and raised the dagger;

I often snuck out of the services to go to the kitchen and eat left-over doughnuts; to boldly explore empty, shadowy halls when I should have been dutifully in a pew -- and the library,

Here's what I wrote to the pastor: "Thanks for the tribute to my father! He would be gratified that his mission being a Sunday School teacher would inspire a child to pursue pastor-hood. I posted your column on Facebook and many family and friends added their input. Your words took me back to when I, too, attended that Sunday School room on the third floor; I was reminded of my father instructing us to pull our chairs into a circle where we could better communicate with each other. In my youth I spent so much time in those buildings -- Sunday services, Wednesday meal and service. I also spent much time exploring those long, shadowy halls while the congregation was elsewhere; my love of reading books took root in that tiny library on the second floor. I'm smiling, just now remembering a poster in the choir room that said "Let's Stay for Church!" but the L looked more like a P. Thanks for prodding those memories!"

Dog Rescue Puts Me Into A State Of Bliss

I climb into the pens with our Rescue dogs and, yes, it's unorthodox and I've heard "Are you up for adoption, too?" 1,296 times.

Most Rescue events have volunteers sitting around playing on their devices while their unhappy dogs are stuck in claustrophobic cages. At an event with my first group, set up on a wintry Saturday afternoon outside an Atlanta PetSmart, I took a brown-and-white dog to potty and, instead of sticking her back in a crate, I sat on a cold metal chair and the 50-pound pit mix immediately jumped into my lap. Hugging her to keep her from falling, it was as if God spoke to me – that this is how the dogs should be shown.

When I first started with Bullywags, everyone looked at me as if I were crazy when I climbed into the exercise pen and sat with the dogs.

My arms have dripped blood, not from bites but from paws of frolicking pups. I almost always feel in a state of bliss, closer to the love of God, in those pens, even when cleaning poop from the floor. Ah, my legs just went numb from sitting so long with a 60 pound white pittie named Trooper happy in my lap, but my soul is jumping from cloud to cloud where I can almost feel the eyes on me, peering through the gate of heaven, their tails wagging.

Back stage Alice Cooper Concert

I was back stage covering the Alice Cooper concert, maybe at the Omni in 1975, when I was a newspaper reporter. In the press area a roadie rolled in a cooler of iced-down Bud (Alice's drink of choice). After the concert he dashed off stage; someone tossed him a towel for his rolling sweat, and he screamed: "I feel like I just went 20 rounds with Muhammad Ali!"

Woolworth's Lunch Counter Next To Book Racks

The closest I usually got to the Greenbriar Woolworth's lunch counter was seeing it through the book racks. While I flipped through Ray Bradbury, Issac Asimov, and Arthur C. Clarke, wondering if I could afford the 25 cents cover price, I recall hearing the metal utensils click against the dishes, smelled the coffee brew, and hamburgers sizzling with onions on the griddle.

Grand Piano In Housing Project

It was the first – and the last – time I'd ever seen a grand piano in an Atlanta housing project.

As an APD investigator, I was assigned to the Housing Authority (AHA) for two years. Atlanta had 42 housing projects and I'd been in most of them:

East Lake Meadows was a violent place, even the residents called it Little Vietnam; others had such an evil miasma that neither grass or trees or bushes grew there.

But one was on Cheshire Bridge Rd NE and was so nice, I'd never suspected it was a project. They were having multiple thefts from rooms – rooms, I quickly learned, where the residents were mostly Russian and German immigrants.

I ended up arresting one AHA security guard for all the thefts. The elated residents, through an interpreter who lived there, were so happy, I was invited over for tea. One elderly Russian lady had a few of her possessions from the homeland, one of which was a beautiful, glistening grand piano which she proudly played for me: Tchaikovsky, Beethoven, turning often to look at me and smile as her arthritic fingers flickered – allegro, glissando – over those beloved keys.

Anxiety Dreams of a Retired Cop

Just dreamed I was back at Inservice and suddenly realized I was still sprawled in the bleachers while every other cop was already firing and I hadn't even gotten my ammo or target.

Anxiety dreams of a retired cop. I often dream of lining up for roll call in uniform, and suddenly realize I am barefoot. Or going to a call I can't remember, and realizing I have no radio with me. Or going to roll call and everyone else are young cops unknown to me; an old timer shows up and says "I remember you!" Or getting in a shootout, but before I can tap tap the trigger, my service weapon falls to pieces in my grip. All my retired cop friends have these, too.

Chasing Fireflies As Kids

Dusk, when I was a kid, was when we leaped and jumped to catch these flying stars. Lightning bugs! Fire flies!

Bad Drivers Test Me As I Go To Church

Inevitably when I am driving to church, I will be tested. Some crazed driver will zip in front of me, then putter along at a Florida-retiree's speed. Non-ecclesiastical words are about to shoot from my mouth but I know heaven is watching, so I put my bazooka back down and, instead, I repeatedly – and loudly – hum hymn after hymn until I am safely ensconced in the back row pew of the balcony in my Fayetteville church.

Rookie Me Arrests A Grandmother

When I was a rookie APD cop I saw the city I'd grown up in in a new, behind-the-scenes, often tragic way.

My FTO (Field Training Officer) responded to a signal 45-holding at the Sears building on Ponce de Leon. The store was bustling with shoppers and I felt like I was masquerading in my new blue uniform (a recurring dream I would have the rest of my life).

A display of yellow Mary Jane candies caught my eye, making me recall going to the store with my Aunt Myrt (still alive on that distant Saturday afternoon); she always bought a bag of this and kept it in a decorative jar, near her parakeet cage, in her Jefferson Ave home.

My FTO went straight to the security office, hidden down a hall where the public was not allowed. Sitting in a chair was an angry woman my aunt's age. What crime could this granny have done? I wondered; surely there's some mistake here.

"Shoplifting?" my FTO assumed.

"Yep," said the security guard, an APD detective working an extra-job. "Another one."

When we helped the sobbing matron into the urine-smelling wagon to be transported to jail, my FTO saw my shocked expression and explained: "It is sad. Old folks work all their lives expecting their golden years will reward them for their life of hard work. But livin' on social security is often a struggle. Never what they expected it would be, so some, like her, rationalize it's ok to steal. They deserve stuff. We gotta go give the security guy a subpoena for her court date."

Passing the display of Mary Janes, I had to look away or else I'd see my aunt.

Old East Point Library

Parking my bike out front, tugging the big outside door open, drifting in the alcove, through one more door -- and I knew I had entered another world. A world of silence where everyone whispered as if Noise would shatter this delicate world.

The old East Point library smelled of ancient paper and the mysterious glue that healed wounded book covers. Ceilings so high cumulonimbus might float up there. Brown window slats spread shafts of sunlight where dust motes swirled in the air conditioner's jet streams.

My pudgy fingers held worlds of imagination -- Ray Bradbury! Issac Asimov! -- read at tables big enough for giants!

TV Dinners Exotic Food

My father became the cook when I was 4 and my mother died. She had made meals of fried chicken and special birthday cakes heavy on icing and love; but my father, the bread-winner unused to doing "woman's work", was more a warmer-upper than a cook. Every day, with almost no exceptions, he served me a wiener on white loaf bread, SpaghettiOs, and Campbell's cream of tomato soup. They were ok but it was like the little black-and-white TV in our lonely living room while our neighbors all had color.

Then one day his oven-mitted hand laid before me a silver rectangle; as he peeled the foil away, my freckled nose feasted, as did my eyes, upon food that *resembled* home-cooked meals: Swanson TV dinners! My favorite was chopped steak that I dipped into Heinz 57 Sauce; that was followed by fried chicken (mostly just crust stuck to chicken bones); roast turkey in white gravy; and roast beef in brown gravy; I soon learned the joy of soaking a slice of white loaf bread in those gravies! They came with mashed potatoes and buttered corn! A BROWNIE for dessert! "Exotic" food was welcomed in that lonely house, where the only hugs I got were from my first dog Flip and from visiting, teary-eyed aunts from my mother's family.   If you have a mom, hug her. Tight.

We Kids Played In Creeks

When I was Huck Finn's age, I lived in a house on DeLowe Dr not 60 yards from a small stream running through woods. We boys dammed up this creek, played War in it. One of my friend's dad hung a tire swing that we could ride swinging over this stream.

In these waters was a monster the older boys called CRAAAYFISH! They had eyes on stalks and pinchers that could snap even a fat boy like me in half! When I finally confronted one of these horrors, no bigger than my thumbnail, I had to use my hyperactive imagination when telling the tale. "The poelice had to go in the woods and kill that crayfish before it escaped and destroyed East Point!"

Psycho Cyclone

I both draw and write and when I was a kid I constructed comic books. That's what I was doing when the psycho cyclone hit my house. I was 11 when a series of crashes and breaking glass came through my bedroom door; my Boston terrier Judy lay nestled against me on the bed; her black ears perked and she started barking.

Following the sound, I saw my stepmother Sara in the living room, breaking furniture, throwing tea glasses against the wall, grabbing everything loose and tossing it in an insane hokey-pokey.

Judy started barking at this huge crazy woman and she stopped, pivoting her torso toward us, her face suffused with anger as she shouted through crooked yellow teeth: "Shut that mutt up or I'll kill it!"

My father was at work; he was a postman delivering mail somewhere in south Atlanta. I was on my own and this made me more terrified than ever at this devil woman. Grabbing the still-barking Judy, I ran out the front door and crossed busy DeLowe Dr, seeking help from neighbors.

"Dad's at work and Sara's tearin' the house up! Said she'd kill Judy!"

My friend's father, Gerry, snarled; he was a Pall Mall-smoking, Schlitz-drinking, motorcycle riding, pool hall denizen who did not like Sara. He lit another Pall Mall and blew smoke like a train as he strode to my house. Leaving Judy safely with Gerry's wife, who never stopped washing dishes in her sink, I followed him at a distance.

"Come out here, you stupid bitch!" Gerry shouted and I took steps backward when I saw her step onto our cement porch. "I ain't scared uh you like Joe is, I'll kick yore gawdamn ass!" Sara bowed up and Gerry rushed to her, shouting cuss words I'd never heard before, his greasy red pompadour shining in the morning light, and Sara deflated. I'd never seen her confronted before. She backed down, despite a look on her face like a cobra's.

Muttering words I couldn't hear, she walked unsteadily to her car and escaped. Gerry angrily dragged on his Pall Mall, burning the filter, obviously wishing she'd tried to fight him.

Gerry's wife called the post office and told them Mr. Cartwright needed to get to his house right away. When we entered together, the place looked like a cyclone – a psycho cyclone – had hit our home. Everything was busted; Gospel records, paper, books, my uncompleted comic book, clothes from drawers, were thrown everywhere.

It was my first stepmother's way of announcing she was divorcing my father.

Lap therapy with new scared pup

Lap therapy. The first Rescue who jumped into my lap was a 60-lb pittie. Wrapping my arms around her lest she fell, she kissed me, and suddenly I realized something very profound just happened.

At a recent Sunday's adoption event, Belle, just Rescued from death row, growled at sweet Bernie because he discovered a piece of treat on the PetSmart floor. Homeless dogs suffer the cold and often must fight just for garbage to eat, and Belle might thus have food aggression.

Taking the leash from her foster, I lifted Belle into my lap and wrapped my arms around her. She seemed to enjoy that love and protection and stayed there a long, contented time. For dogs who've known only unhappiness, lap is pal spelled backward.

Childhood metal foot measuring device

My father took me to Buster Brown Shoes in Campbellton Plaza where the salesman took off my sneaker and put my foot into this metal contraption, looked like a beaver trap from the Daniel Boone TV show. Slides slid on both sides of my foot. My toe, cold where it peeked out of a hole in my sock and touched the metal device, stopped at a number on a scale, and that was my shoe size.

Someone on the *What's My Line?* TV show I watched with my great-Aunt Myrt, while we sat on her sofa, next to her tables of colorful porcelain knick-knacks, and ate candy orange wedges, tried to stump the panel. He made these foot-measuring devices from our childhood, and Mr Charles Daly, the show's moderator, called it a Brannock device.

Wingo's Steak

When I got my first car, one of the places I frequented was Wingo's restaurant on Campbelton Rd. Just in 10th grade at Headland HS, I had to count my coins to pay my check and a very little for a tip.

The silver salad dressing holder at Wingo's looked like Mr Spock's 3D chess set; it held 3 open bowls of bleu cheese, French, and Thousand Islands. I always ordered the KC steak with french fries ($2.50) and extra Wingo's sauce. I dipped my steak and those tasty wheat rolls into that mysterious black sauce.

What You See On The Street

People ask me to describe what you see working the streets. I say, you've seen the commercials for medications where they go on and on listing possible side effects: nausea, dementia, paranoia, suicidal tendencies, and homicidal tendencies. Yeah, that pretty much sums it up.

Work With Netherlands Police At 1996 Olympics

During the 1996 Summer Olympics in Atlanta, I worked with three cops from Gooi en Vechtstreek, a region in the Netherlands.

There was a lot of down time for us so we talked a lot. Compared to crime-fighting in Atlanta, their experience was almost bucolic; they didn't carry a firearm; they rode bicycles; and their criminals sounded quite polite compared to ours.

They thought they'd get to see America for free by electing to be attached to the Olympics police; instead, they were stuck in a hole with us at the Omni coliseum.

One of the visiting cops was named Heidi, a buxom, pouty beauty. The guy was named Marten. I don't recall the nice but plain-looking female officer's name. Maybe Heidi was so pouty because all the Atlanta cops kept hitting on her. Did I mention Heidi was a Dutch hottie?

Cashing in empties to buy candy

Empty bottles rattling in the wire basket of my red bike as I peddled up DeLowe to Harris Jr. We kids would prowl the sidewalks looking for empty pop bottles that we would cash in at the corner store...usually just pennies' worth. We also bought Ugly Stickers to stick on our lunch boxes...back in the 60's. Maybe a mixed Slushee and Sugar Babies, too.

Cass Licks My Hand As I Try To Write Something Sad

As I scribble sad words with a pencil, my white boxer Cassie starts licking my hand, making my scribbles unreadable. Oh, well, I laugh, looking at her silly, happy face. I wasn't writing anything important, any way. Let's play!

Do Some Street People Prefer That Life?

Who in their right mind would trade a safe bed for a concrete curb as a pillow?

Most people who find themselves suddenly homeless are thankful to find safe shelter and food, but on my beat in downtown Atlanta in 1978 I discovered some who would literally fight to remain homeless.

One was Stan. His sister flagged me down in my patrol car one hot summer night on Ponce.

"I'm trying to get my brother Stan to come home with me, but he won't. Can you make him come with me?"

I knew Stan. The last few months he'd been foraging from dumpsters behind some Peachtree St restaurants while sleeping in the dirt basement of an abandoned house that reeked of booze-soaked human waste. He was different in that he spoke intelligently, like a college professor, but then rambled off into drunken slurring.

"He was a successful business man," his sister told me that night under the neon streetlight, "but he let booze get the better of him."

I went with her to talk to him. He seemed 30 with black rim glasses with the right lens bisected by a grimy crack. She beseeched her brother, grabbing his arm, but he cursed her and told her to get out of his life.

When she left, he confided in me that, living on the street, he had a freedom he preferred. Eventually I realized I hadn't seen Stan in a while.

Then there was Wally, a country boy who'd come to Hotlanta for some Saturday night fun. He paid a PDL hooker named Celeste and was so blown away by the experience, he stayed on the street, becoming a drug addict. One night I realized I hadn't seen Wally for a while.

Celeste had come from the country, too. She was once pretty, unlike most street hookers, but her trip to the big city ended with her addicted to Dilaudid. Over many months, the street life, and addiction, destroyed her good looks. Eventually I realized I hadn't seen Celeste in a while.

Living on the street is hard as a concrete pillow.

Stan was unique in that he could articulate the perverse sense of freedom living on the street gave him. No expectations, just a feral day-to-day existence.

Cripple Woman Swims

The young woman swimming in the public pool was amazing – zipping from one end to the other, underwater and then above water. I was retired and swimming in this covered Clayton County pool was part of my exercise.

Yet she had hobbled to the edge of the pool on aluminum crutches with arm cuffs; her back and legs stiff and slow, suggesting a condition, not an injury she could recover from.

She swam with beauty and speed, like a happy dolphin, splashing, buoyant, weightless!

Climbing out of the pool, each painful step up slowed her. Hurt her. Her aluminum crutches clanking as I watched her squint back down at the calm, blue water, as if looking from this world into another world.

Rescue Samson climbs into restroom stall

I had to visit the restroom while at the PetSmart dog adoption event.

I had Rescue Sampson on the leash, so I took him with me. Inside takin' care of business, I was not watching Sammy, when I heard a voice from inside the next stall say: "Well, hello, fella!" and I realized Sammy had climbed under the stall wall and some guy was in there.

"Sorry!" I said.

"No problem," said the voice. "This is going to make an interesting post!"

So, if you read on social media about an 80-lb pittie coming into a stall while the guy's inside using it, it REALLY happened. I know. I was there!

Charles Chips Delivered

After a roast beef lunch at Cracker Barrel I spotted a bag of Charles Chips in their store and it opened memories: when I was a kid, one of our neighbors had Charles Chips in a tin barrel delivered to their door; me and other kids gathered and watched this novelty.

Charles Chips was special, better'n store-bought; when I tasted some, at our neighbor's, I convinced myself they were better'n what my family bought at Harris Jr's. So I snatched the bag off the shelf and looked forward to snacking on it while watching cable that evening.

When I ripped the bag open, I half-expected unicorns to fly out as I dug in. It was ok, but I won't stop buying Lays.

Church Donuts

Fat boy loved donuts! After Sunday school, and before the 11 o'clock church service at East Point First Methodist Church, when I was a fat boy, I'd make a beeline to the then-empty kitchen.

Earlier in the morning, they would warm donuts in the oven (no microwaves Back Then!) and serve them with coffee to the sleepy-eyed flock.

I'd search the kitchen and happily munch all left-over donuts, even the ones turning hard. Fat boy loved donuts!

Drug Store Grill

As a fat East Point kid on a bicycle, I loved biking to a drug store in the Headland / DeLowe shopping center where I discovered I could order a hamburger from the grill for a quarter (from my allowance) and crinkle-cut French fries, or a hot dog for a dime. I first saw purple onions at that grill.

APD chaplain rides with me

"One of the APD chaplains wants to do a ride-along with you," my sarge, with a porn star mustache, told me;

I patrolled the Peachtree Street Strip in 1978. "His church is on your beat. Introduce him to the whores and pimps and junkies!"

I, the son of a Methodist Sunday School teacher, believe the hand of God has shielded me from bullets and bombs as well as knives, rocks, and fists aimed at me. APD had several chaplains, they wore an honorary Captain's uniform; one, an

Orthodox rabbi, had a full beard and forelocks in his uniform. I couldn't tell what church this chaplain represented; he was young, clean-shaven with short, dark hair and reminded me of a Headland HS science teacher who kept a Milky Way bar tucked into his shirt pocket.

For two hours I introduced him to beat 207, at the time the city's smallest, but most active, beat.

"If you know these are prostitutes," he asked from the passenger seat, "why don't you arrest them?"

"We can't arrest them unless we hear them proposition someone. A potential customer would be directed to a dark alley where the deal would go down."

"*In*-teresting."

Around 2 AM, yawning, he thanked me and said it was past his bedtime. "But I will sleep securely knowing there are brave officers like you keeping us safe!"

Returning him to his car, we passed the Unification church on my beat, and I said, "Now, there's a nut religion. The Moonies."

"*In*-teresting."

At the end of the watch, my sarge asked "How'd the Moonie chaplain like his ride-along with you?"

I froze. "He's a Moonie?"

"I didn't tell you?" the sarge asked, Krispy Kreme doughnut bits in his porn star mustache.

Every time that chaplain saw me after that ride-along, he'd rush over, shake my hand and ask how I was.

David Mitchell's Chess Set

When I was a kid in East Point, I and my buddies with mud in our sneaker soles from wading in the nearby creek, each had a cheap plastic chess set.

One day one of the older boys, David Mitchell, proudly showed us snot-nosed kids what his parents just bought him: a chess set of carved wood pieces, glistening and lovely, smooth to my pudgy fingers. His didn't play any better than mine, but, gosh, were they pretty!

EP Pool high dive

The East Point pool had a dive, a high dive, and a *hiiiiiiiiiiigh* dive.

My first try at it consisted of a long line, then kids waiting on the ladder. When I finally scaled that Matterhorn, I recall looking earthward and that massive pool now looked the size of a matchbox.

I shook in spasms of fear, looking down at the tops of trees. I could see my house three miles away! A high-altitude wind pushed my young body back, back, making the kids on the ladder think I was chicken to jump. They hurled epithets at me that no child of East Point should have used. Since they backed down the ladder, I decided to go that way, and descended through the clouds.

Head lowered, I hurried through the hooting crowd and took solace in an orange push-up at the snack bar.

Elementary school had same librarian for 112 years

There was only one librarian at Conley Hills, my elementary school for 112 years. She must have had some very interesting tomes hidden in her office!

Do dogs have a soul?

Do dogs have a soul? I've looked into the eyes of so many dogs, dogs who suffered and love healed them, and the love they had was clear and sure in those eyes looking into my soul.

How could I doubt that they do? Some argue God only instilled a soul into humans, but God breathed life into all living things, a divine act. In heaven, the Bible says, the lion shall lay down with the lamb. Dog is God spelled backward. In Rescue, we constantly deal with abused dogs and we use the power of Love to undo the evil done to them. As for cats, I am unable to decide.

Red Light On My Curtain

The revolving red light pulsed in our driveway, behind the Lone Ranger curtain in my room, then the window was dark until the next revolving flash, like heart beats.

I was 4, awakened by crying and shrill shouting in our house, so I stood in the corner of my crib, mesmerized by my curtain turning red, then black, then red, not knowing it was a revolving red light stuck by a magnet to the onyx roof of a local hearse, in a time when East Point had no ambulances, but paid funeral homes to transport the sick and injured to the nearest hospital in north Atlanta.

I was too young to understand when the red light receded from my curtain, like a heart stopping; and my mother's next ride, in that long, black car, would not require use of the red light.

Dreams of Magical Flying

I step up into the starry sky, then leap as if from a super-high diving board, and I am flying! Above the treetops. Tempted to peer, voyeur-like, into un-curtained windows.

All my life I've magically flown. In dreams, of course. The one I remember most is gliding above a sparkling beach and out over the ocean. I can see into the dark depths, amazed at all the mysterious life there, deep in that subconscious sea.

Often when my feet leave the earth, I have to dip and duck to avoid hitting power lines as I ascend. When I awake I am elated, ecstatic, wishing I really could do like the birdies do.

Stripper Transformation

Her stripper name was Tiffany. But, before her perhaps Faustian transformation, decades ago, we knew her at Manuel's Tavern as Becky; I may remember the names wrong, but that's not important. She tore off her old persona as deftly as she doffed her clothes on the Tattletale's stage.

As Becky, she was shy and quiet with mousey-brown hair and colorless clothes. Word was she entered, and won, an amateur strip contest.

When "Tiffany" first made her grand entrance at Manuel's, she shone like the stage lights were still on her; her hair was now blonde and sassy; her clothes, no doubt held together by Velcro, was tight and showed off her surgically-altered cleavage. She was all flash and haughty laughter, and soon we never saw her again.

I thought about catching one of her performances, but never did. I assume she grew tired of a world where we all chose to wear clothes.

East Point Pool

Let me count the ways. I loved the East Point pool because I was little and it was gigantic – a man-made cement lake sparkling like a mirage on a summer day.

For a nickel or a dime, I could freeze my tongue with a peach push-up; or a frozen Milky Way bar on a stick; or delicious, stale, butter popcorn.

The outside jukebox blasted songs, usually "Wooly Bully" while Ronnie Ray danced to it over and over again.

There were older women in bikinis (14 or 15!), who I was too shy to look at directly.

But I loved to swim – the shallow to the deep end like a southside Moby Dick. Above water I could hear my friends calling out to each other, and I could hear "Wooly Bully"; but submerging, all was watery silence, like I was back in amniotic fluid, and if I listened hard enough, I'd hear the thoughts of God.

Back to the surface, I felt like I could tread water in that magical pool – forever!

Duchess Fostered

I opened the door of my white car and Duchess jumped in. That was the start of a hundred field trips with this sweet Rescue and me.

Everywhere we went, people loved this plotthound-pit mix, played with her, and got kissed by her. Soon she insisted on crawling in my lap as I drove. She loved being out but hated being returned to her kennel; she became stressed, suffering from Shelter Syndrome.

Another volunteer, Jamie, talked her neighbor Frank into meeting Duchess. To know Duchess is to love her and Frank fell under her spell and agreed to foster. I was happy, but missed my baby and paid them a visit after a few days.

Sitting on the carpet, Duchess wiggled in my lap again. She now had a home to play in, and was especially fond of naps on the sofa. The first time Frank awoke with Duchess asleep on his chest, he knew she was right for him and he adopted the sweet baby.

They went for daily walks.

They walked with me to my car. I opened the door and Duchess pulled on the leash to jump in. She looked at me, then at Frank. They went up the sidewalk and I slammed shut the door of my white car.

Fernbank Planetarium And Razzles

I associate Antares, the Milky Way, and the rings of Saturn with Razzles rasberry candy.

I remember, as a kid, totally mesmerized watching the Fernbank planetarium shows, mouth agape as I shoveled Razzles into it.

The lecturer had a melodious German accent as he spoke over the background music, which was classical. Looking at the stars projected onto the dome, I felt my body levitating through the cosmos. I associate the planetarium with Razzles. First it's candy. Then it's gum. The wonders of science!

Fight In Headland Boys Room

Word spread quickly: during the next break between classes, there was going to be a fight in the boys room closest to Mrs. Bussey's English classroom. Two tenth graders, I don't remember who or why, were going to settle some dispute known only to them.

After the bell, boys filled the restroom, must have been 70 guys crowding in, several climbing to perch atop the ceramic stall walls.

One combatant entered, then the other and the crowd closed in around them, forming a little oval arena. They glared hatefully at each other and muttered words I was too far away to hear.

"Fight!"

"Do it, already!" fellow students taunted.

Of all the fights I'd seen in East Point, two guys would usually push each other, or wrestle, then their friends would break it up, and it was over. Not this time. One boy let fly a barrage of fists, brutal, almost professional, and when the other boy spun to escape, I saw his right eye swollen, and escape through the crowd impossible. Lucky for him, two coaches, who no doubt noticed not a single male student in the entire building, kicked through the door and penetrated the now escaping crowd, to break up the fight.

As I fled in that wave, back this way or that to 8th grade art class, the sudden brutality numbed me. Like it was I who had been hit.

Hear Fire And Rain On Radio At Night

My alarm was set to Radio and came on, awakening me for 10th grade homeroom. Opening my eyes, hearing this song for the first time, the lyrics resonated with the angst in my teenage soul, there in my bed buried in pre-dawn night. As the song played, I really thought I did, indeed, have a friend in this dark, cold, scary world.

Hear Jody's Radio When I Was A Kid, Shared Bedroom

My little dog Flip had just died. My brother was 16 years older than me; when I was around 4 we shared a bedroom in our East Point home.

I vividly remember being awakened and hearing my brother falling into his bed and the hurt-soul tune of "Rag Doll" lilting from his AM clock radio. As I dozed back to sleep, the falsetto words of The Four Seasons spun my dream: a lonely girl alone on a street as a cold storm soaked her, but she was too sad to seek cover; the cold rain was her tears. Poor Dawn. Poor me.

High beam incivility

I was a little kid watching my dad drive the family car one night.

"What choo doin', Daddy?" I studied his face as he squinted in the lights from the high beams of an approaching car.

"I just flashed my headlights because the car approaching forgot he was driving with his high beams on. He must've forgot and he turned 'em off. High-beams blind the driver in the approaching car."

"Oh," I said, nodding like an adult. That was fifty or so years ago. You do the same thing now and the approaching driver thinks nothing of your polite gesture; most don't care if they are blinding you. High-beam incivility; courtesy may not be dead in our time, but it is certainly on life-support.

He Who Fights Monsters Me In Serial Killer School

Whoever fights monsters may become one, Nietzsche once warned.

Having fought evil as an APD cop, and as a volunteer working with abused Rescue dogs, I've seen that those blue knights are less likely to become a monster than to become its victim, their body and soul chewed with fangs and burned with the dragon's fire.

As a Homicide detective, I was sent to the FBI's Serial Killer school. We studied crime scene photos of unimaginable brutality (serial killers are usually intelligent, evil, and attracted to ritualistic brutality).

I turned my head when a cop in the desk beside me had to rest his head on his arms to keep from fainting at those horrid photos.

During a break, one of the profilers, prematurely gray and deeply puffing a hot cigarette, nervously looking over his shoulder as if fearful of a lurking attacker, told me: "I have strict rules for my family. If they are not home, they have to call me *every* two hours. Once, my teenage daughter was out shopping with a friend, and forgot to call. I know what kind of evil monsters are out there, so I feared the worst. I was freaking out, ready to grab my weapon and go looking for her. She finally called me, crying as she apologized, because she knew how her missed call would effect me." Grinding out his cigarette with trembling, yellowed fingers, he called the class back in session.

Taking my seat, I was not surprised to see the desk next to me was now empty. Gaze into the abyss and you can imagine the devil's eyes. Watching YOU.

Housing Projects Where Even Grass Won't Grow

Most of Atlanta's 42 housing projects were moderately pleasant places, but three I worked in seemed so evil that grass and trees planted there promptly died; the poisonous ground was like the surface of the moon; shattered liquor bottles glistened in the parking lots like icy patches; and every outside door and window were barred like prisons because of the criminal legions living there among the decent folks they victimized. Kids gleefully chased pitiful stray dogs while stoning them. The average age of a grandmother was 32.

In 1997, APD transferred me to the Atlanta Housing Authority. To ready myself, I read the contract that all residents must sign. It stated any family could be expelled from the AHA dole for criminal activity. Instead of criminal court, my seasoned partner and I specialized in evicting criminals and it started making that bad land more of a kind place. The AHA director launched a plan razing most of the projects and building mixed-income developments where the remaining inhabitants lived next-door to students and young professionals. The blighted grass and trees became green and alive after a long, long hibernation.

I As Kid Alone See TZ Gremlin On TV

"Don't you get out of bed," my father warned me before closing my bedroom door with finality. "We'll be back in less than an hour!"

I was probably 8 and he and my evil first stepmother left me home alone. Of course I shot out of bed like a rocket as soon as I saw their car lights, on my Lone Ranger curtain, pull down our driveway.

Our huge cabinet TV, in the dark, silent living room, took minutes to "warm up", the ancient tubes sizzling and cooing. And suddenly there with me was this horrid close-up picture of the gremlin from the Twilight Zone, mere inches from my chubby face.

In tears, I fled back to the protecting covers of my bed, leaving the flickering evidence of my crime. What scared me most was how much the gremlin reminded me of my evil stepmother!

I Expose Psychic On Boortz Show

The angry psychic glared at me from my TV screen and hissed: "Steve. I see you havin' a TERRIBLE accident. You need to be extra careful around dark cars!"

This was around 1976 and Neal Boortz had a local TV show on, as I recall, UHF channel 36. I didn't know him, but he'd read some of my articles in *The Atlanta Constitution* (pre-AJC) and *Creative Loafing* about things psychic.

He had a local psychic scheduled who said she could do clairvoyant readings to callers on the air. He wanted me to help him expose her fakery. From home, I watched the show unfurl on my little BW TV. After the "psychic" "read" me, Boortz introduced me and asked: "Steve, did she get anything right?"

"No," I said, at which time the psychic issued her thinly veiled threat against me. It's been over 40 years and her prediction has yet to come true.

I Fight Dream Demon

At 2 AM your soul seems as dark as the night.

In my bed, I sensed a great evil force in my room, and it paralyzed me with fear as it drew closer.

Crying out, moving in slow motion, I wanted to escape as I saw, in a dark corner, a mist starting to take shape; it sparked and swirled like evil smoke, silent lightning bolts cracking, probably a childhood memory, filed away in my subconscious library, of watching an Outer Limits episode as a child. Run, run, run!

Suddenly something told me to stop and FIGHT! Reluctantly I turned, fists trembling, and the thing drew close enough to touch, when it froze, as if uncertain. It jumped up and down as if in a temper tantrum, but when I did not flee, the demon burst into a million pieces whose dark fire extinguished.

A surfer's wave of joy and triumph washed me from the dark subconscious sea onto a sunny beach. Seeing I was safe in my warm bed, I realized the significance of this dream: stand up and fight and your fear will blow away and leave you alone.

Headland Lunches

By the time I galloped into the second floor of the circular Headland HS cafeteria, sniffing the air for something familiar, looking at the plates for clues, my teenaged stomach was *hongry!*

I'd check out the main meal serving table but usually exited stage left for the sandwich line. I still smile when thinking of the pizza, even though all it was was dough, ground hamburger with cheese, and I had to baptize it in ketchup to make it resemble pizza. Or the po boy sandwich that no one in Louisiana would recognize. Or the chip dip I made by mixing mustard and ketchup!

I Forget My Pants Going To Church

Yes, I missed church last Sunday. It's a 35 minute drive to Fayetteville and I was almost there when I realized I wasn't wearing my pants. Another senior moment. I couldn't go like that. I'll be there next Sunday, if I don't forget what day it is. I always wear jogging shorts, but when going to church I put black jogging pants over the jogging shorts; after church, I pull off the pants and go to my Rescue event.

I Have A Touch Of OCD

I've never been diagnosed with it, but I suspect I have a touch of OCD. When my mother died my developing brain has ever since equated loving someone or some thing with death and separation. Every time I leave my house, I'm thinking it could catch fire or a sinkhole swallow it. Driving my car invokes images of a Mack truck doing to me what Wile E. Coyote tried to do to Road Runner.

I no longer live in that troubled house, but *it* continues to live in me.

If you have similar obsessions, ye are not alone – Let us drink a toast together, of the dark, and bitter, ale that Life has poured for us!

I see UFO With My Telescope As A Kid

"Fernbank's been getting *hundreds* of UFO sightings!"

When I was about 5, I lay on my back and contemplated the stars. When I felt like I was drifting up to those stars, I ran into my parent's house in East Point. I was gifted a toy telescope a few years later. I trembled, not from the winter air, but from seeing the moon's surface so close, like my Keds were on one of those hills.

Suddenly a light seemed to fly from the moon. My knees were wobbly as my telescope followed it till it flew behind the neighbor's trees.

"I saw a FLYING SAUCER!" I screamed, running into my house. My father, after several busy signals, reported it to Fernbank Science Center in Decatur.

"We've turned this over to the Air Force," the harried secretary said. At 2 AM, someone from the Air Force called to say we'd all seen the Telstar satellite. Was it another government cover-up?

I steal a Playboy

The Playboys for April 1969 were displayed near the chain-smoking cashier at the book store at Greenbriar mall and I was determined to steal one.

I was 13 and too embarrassed to attempt to buy it, even if the law allowed it, but something told me there were pictures in there that I needed to see! So, with sweat pouring, I casually plucked one and scurried to a secluded aisle where I stuck it under my shirt, tucking my shirt in so it wouldn't fall out and reveal my dastardly crime.

Clumsily, I dropped the money for the purloined Playboy near where the cashier turned his back to snub out his cigarette, and I ran into the busy mall!

Once home, I locked my bedroom door and flopped on my unmade bed, opening the magazine with chubby, trembling fingers. And see, I did, golly gee willikers!

Then guilt swatted me, my conscience exclaiming: "Just what are you doing! No one has ever done anything as dastardly as this!" I thought of Edgar Alan Poe's "The Telltale Heart" where a murderer thinks he can hear his dead victim's heart beating from its concealment, proclaiming his crime to all! My heart, too, was pounding!

Unable to bear it, I wrapped the thing in newspapers intended for the Conley Hills Elementary paper drive, and again concealed it under my shirt! Pedaling my red bike, I ditched the thing into the dumpster behind Harris Jr's little store and sped away, fearful the thing would strip off its papers and run after me, barking at me like a demon dog! Every person I saw must be looking at me as I peddled faster, them knowing my sin!

Even in my escape, I was subconsciously planning the next theft of a future Playboy magazine!

I take David Byron to Underground Atlanta

It sounds glamorous: Rock-and-roll reporter (me) takes rock superstar (David Byron of Uriah Heep) to Underground Atlanta.

I was 18 in 1975; my Headland HS class graduated in '74 but I had to complete one more quarter. I was a reporter for the *South Fulton News-Daily* but sold rock stories to *Creative Loafing* and the *Atlanta Gazette*.

Uriah Heep had a new album about to be released and were on a publicity tour; that's how I had an interview with Byron. The interview over, he said he'd heard about rock bands playing in Underground Atlanta and would I take him to see some? Glamorous. In reality, I was making more money than I ever had, but I was becoming an adult and needed to supplement my check by delivering the newspaper I helped write.

Before the singer could sit in my car, I had to throw 100 rolled *News-Dailies* into the back seat of my rusty, old, blue Impala. In Underground, fans wanting his autograph besieged Byron. In one bar, the singer in the local band recognized the superstar, and stopped singing to rush to our table begging for an autograph.

Soon I was back in East Point, throwing rolled *News-Dailies* out the window of my Impala. Glamorous!

Jaunty exchange in class between teacher and Dodo
Dowda

Dodo: an extinct bird; also what Coach Ellerbee almost daily called select students in his class. One student was "Dodo Dowda!"

They were friendly exchanges that could take place in the early 1970ies, but certainly not today. I could see that student, a known wordsmith, Kim Dowda's brain was self-censoring his words before he shot them off into the Headland HS air.

These exchanges tickled everybody in the classroom, making students smile and laugh, a break from all that book-learnin'; but if it happened in a school today, the teacher would no doubt be fired, pilloried in the press, sued in court, and sentenced to hard labor in Politically Correct Prison.

I won't even mention the coach who taught his class with an unlit cigar jutting from the side of his mouth. We innocently did not suspect that our way of life was even then lumbering toward the tar pits, soon to be as extinct as the proverbial dodo.

Jean Can't Find Her Mom

My friend Jean tells me her father just chopped down a tree in their back yard but she can't tell her mother because Jean can't find her mom.

Jean was 88 and had had Alzheimer's over a year When she told me something I knew wasn't true -- like children were running and whooping through her house -- I wanted to correct her, to tell her there's no kids there, that her parents are . . . long dead.

That would be the wrong thing to tell her, I kept telling myself. And no, getting her to admit the truth wouldn't reverse her illness. So I listened to her pa chopping the tree story. For the hundredth time. I'm just glad I could still hear Jean's voice, no matter what she's telling me.

Let's go look at hippies

"Let's go look at hippies!" my first step-mother exclaimed in our East Point home in 1966 when I was 10, and the family piled into the station wagon and headed for The Strip in downtown Atlanta. Six Flags Over Georgia had not yet opened, and The Strip may have foreshadowed Lion Country Safari where customers drove their car through a compound of captive exotic animals.

A few blocks on Peachtree Street around 10th Street had become a hippy enclave and hippies did not look like the kind of folk who you sat near in church, or played ball with at Grayson field, or politely waved to at Morrison's cafeteria. They had long hair and beards (and that was the women!) and dressed in bohemian clothes they called threads; hippies playing frisbee in the middle of Peachtree St.; runaways were drawn there; aspiring musicians hung out there; drug addicts stumbled along the sidewalks and were found dead in its dirty alleys at sunrise.

And suburbanites drove there to look, point, and laugh.

I'd heard tour buses went there regularly, for a fee.

Likely only dogs will mourn my passing

I will likely only have dogs mourning my ultimate passing, whenever that may be. That's OK, except they'll need help crossing the street.

Magic 8 Ball

When I was a kid, we got direct guidance from the spirit world. But you had to first come into possession of the mystical Magic 8 Ball!

Math teacher enigmatically gives English lesson

Enigma in my 8th grade Math class. Mrs Coralee Gunn did not mention hypotenuses, or integers; she, in her sweet, southern drawl, declared that day in 1970: "When trying to remember how many s's it takes to spell 'dessert' and 'desert', just remember which one of them you want more of!" I have remembered, and utilized, this proverb my entire, long life!

May be last intuitive doctor

The doctor accented his words by waving his index finger like a magic wand and heartily laughing when I affirmed his clairvoyance was correct.

Years ago, I switched my health care to one of those collectives, and everyone said I should choose Dr Long as my PCP. He was so popular his appointments usually took three months. He was so intuitive I almost felt his psychic energy was X-raying me.

Of course, he quickly left to go into private practice. The other doctors consulted at a computer screen, typing in my symptoms, then caressing the

SUBMIT button. When the computer went down all diagnoses ceased.

But I knew Dr Long was out there somewhere – waving his finger like a magic wand and heartily laughing when his new -- lucky -- patient nodded at his almost supernatural diagnosis.

Jean reads to me like a mother reading fairy tale

Jean was 87 and we'd been friends 10 years.

I still called her daily, and she was so happy to hear from me, thinking we hadn't conversed in months.

It used to be she'd tell me about her day; about making herself lunch, chicken Alfredo, adding a fried egg on top. If she mentioned a misery I knew she was in pain because her Irish upbringing discouraged complaining, valuing a strong perseverance that made her a respected nurse at Georgia Baptist.

Also in her mind, her parents were still alive; her mother visits and plays the piano in the spotless living room full of knickknacks; her husband Al still sneaks into their garage to smoke a cigar. Our conversations were no longer two-sided; inexplicably, she would start reading to me, from some old mail or her church bulletin, in a clear, sing-songy voice like a mother reading a fairy tale to her child.

Me and Rick In HHS Art Class

All my life I knew I was a writer and an illustrator. I dreamed of seeing my name on a big city newspaper masthead as staff writer and cartoonist.

Social Studies and PE were boring chores at Headland High School, but Ms Mandy Wright's Art class was time in a magic tent. In that wonder land she waved her hands, with long and colorful nails, wood bracelets clacking, drawing my imagination into her special light, rain clouds rolling and banging with thunder.

In that class I shared a paint-splotched table with a young Rick Parker. Rick knew his path was to be a commercial artist and he spoke in loud tones about that exotic world so far away from our East Point. Ripping and popping with mysticism and spirituality, I'm convinced his eyes could peer into the future and see himself awarded for projects from such high-end clients as Coke; maybe Rick could even "see" me as I sit here, now, at my computer, gazing back into the past. A past spent at a paint-splotched table inside a wonderfully magical tent.

Me and Bobby misbehave in church balcony

In the church balcony is where it was first revealed to me that I am a contrarian and two chubby little boys can't help but misbehave. A contrarian will laugh if others cry. They -- we -- can't help it.

I was maybe 9 when me and my friend Bobby Brown convinced our parents we were mature enough to sit together in EP First Methodist during morning service at 11, seeking our independence as Dr Spock said pre-adolescents will.

We were alone in the balcony, in the last row, every pious back to us. Except for the choir. We *tried* to be reverent and quiet, but all that reverence demanded reverence from us. Suppress giggling! That's when the giggles started. It didn't help when Bobby made snorting noises while singing from the hymnal and I continued to fight the impious giggles. Suppress! Once someone, especially a kid, starts giggling, there is no stopping. Tears came to our eyes. A lady in the choir did not approve and she got up from the choir section, scurried down the hall, and ascended unto the balcony and sat between me and Bobby, making us fear the punishment that was sure to come. From our parents, and maybe from God, too.

Me As Kid Look At Stars From Car's Back Windshield

I was probably 4, bouncing unrestrained in the family car's back seat, as kids did back then, as my father drove through East Point, both hands on the huge steering wheel.

I looked at the empty space beneath the curving back window and wondered if I could fit in there. Laying there on my back, I looked through the glass at the mysterious points of light and my young brain tried to fathom a cosmos with no end. I could see craters and shadowy shapes on the bright full moon and suddenly felt like the moon was trying to pull me through the window and into its embrace.

Rolling quickly back into the seat, I decided I'd rather stay on Earth.

Memory fails, as I recall

As I've reached a lofty perch of age, I look back at my past while tapping my No. 2 against the waiting keyboard.

Through a glass darkly, a cinema screen with the curtains already closing. Did my favorite Conley Hills elementary teacher drink lipstick-stained cups of coffee from her desk? Did I leave my reporter job in '77 or '78?

As memory becomes elusive like a rabbit scurrying for its hole, I find myself having to throw in several "as I recall" or "my memory of that is . . . " If you read one of my recollections and you don't see one of those caveats – well. I guess I just forgot!

Military influence in East Point

I and countless other boys climbed on the cannon that once reposed proudly in the front yard of East Point city hall, while our dads were inside paying our utility bill.

The military was a major influence in East Point's past. I can still smell the savory BBQ being grilled in the American Legion Post 51 parking lot; inside the building was a community hall. It held several long tables, reminding me of the legend of the afterlife where Viking warriors feasted and told their heroic tales. But the long tables, in that hall always heavy with cigarette and cigar smoke, was where barbecue plates, with Brunswick stew and cold bottles of beer, were consumed.

A red-headed "older" man trudged our streets, clutching a rolled-up newspaper like a cudgel. Rumor was he'd been shell-shocked in WW2 and walked constantly and saluted telephone poles. Our parents warned us to avoid him.

I was called out of class in Headland HS to be interviewed in the circular cafeteria by the Selective Service board who assigned me a lottery number that might send me to Vietnam where I could maybe fire a cannon like the one at city hall. Many a boy who had played on that cannon, the lucky ones, grew old and stooped and got to eat BBQ at the long tables in the American Legion's smoky hall.

Exceptional Rescues That Started Out Rowdy

I have known 5 exceptional dogs in my decade of dog Rescue, including 2 books, but none started well.

When I first met Deja, she tried to escape her crate at an adoption event and I busted my finger stopping her. As I worked one-on-one with her, we finally bonded so strongly that, when I eventually had to hand her leash to her new owner and Deja dragged him as she tried to leave with me, my heart felt like the Hindenburg exploding.

Callie was such a trouble-maker we had to call in Dog Behaviorist Barry Sechler to transform her. She's now a service dog for a wounded Marine and has literally saved his life more than once.

Deuces came to us at Bullywags Rescue with the manners you'd expect from a dog always chained to a tree and beaten and abused by a teenager. Deuces finally got love, and he now kisses everybody he sees.

So don't give up on a seemingly rowdy Rescue until you've given them love, and patience.

Mentioning things from the 60ies

A candy cigarette dangled from my lips as I adjusted the volume on my AM radio, hoping the DJ played my song request so I could record it on my reel-to-reel tape recorder. I was still drinking the bottle of Coke I got at the drive-in.

Yikes, it was late -- Pete the milkman would deliver our bottles of milk soon! Channel 5 played the national anthem and the test pattern came on the screen and that dang DJ still hadn't played my request and I had to be in school real dang soon!

Pepper spray gets me later in court

When the judge saw me break into tears on the front row, she must've thought the sadness of the case touched me. But a fellow APD detective, a lanky Larceny detective sitting next to me as we waited to testify, knew different, and he jumped up and ran out of the courtroom.

APD started using oleoresin capsicum (OC), a spray derived from chili peppers, in the 1990ies, and part of our training was to run through a pink cloud of the hybrid of salsa.

Two hours later I sat, bored, in municipal court and rubbed my tired eyes. A chili particle clinging to my eyelash was now sitting on my eyeball and felt like a zillion hornets stinging me.

The lanky Larceny detective rushed back into the courtroom and dabbed my throbbing eye with a wet paper towel until, seemingly eons later, I could once again open my eyes.

First thing I saw was the judge smiling proudly and nodding at me, no doubt impressed by my empathy for the victim standing before her.

Storm rages outside skyscraper dream-like

Twice I've been high up in a skyscraper while a thunderstorm raged just outside the thin pane of the window.

Thunder rattled the swaying room, reminding me I was 66 stories off the Earth, like a conflicted angel in flight.

Beyond the pane, clouds blew and swirled as lightning rippled and pulsed. Somewhere deep in my subconscious, a cul de sac of the Id resonated, a creative place that magically transforms our inner turmoils into nightmares of fast-approaching storms – tornadoes of the sleeping mind. I knew Thor could hurl a lightning bolt at me, and when the dark sky exploded in green lightning bursts, I stumbled back from the vibrating window, aware I could not so easily step back from that place in my subconscious that disguises our inner turmoil into dream-storms.

My Friend Jean Has Alzheimer's

I think it's time to stop correcting her. My friend Jean, 88, has Alzheimer's. When she tells me she has to find her car and drive home, I've been telling her, "Jean, you *are* home. It's as if I can convince her of what's real – she will be cured.

In her mind, her mama and daddy are still alive and they are a happy family living still in Darian, GA where little Jean goes to the wharf to watch the boats dock, their holds full of shrimp. And she thinks she smells the Vicks VapoRub on her Aunt Polly when Jean naps in her safe, loving lap.

So now when my friend says she has to find her car and drive home, I tell her: "Have a nice drive home, Jean. Tell your Aunt Polly hello for me."

Me As Kid Stand At Rain Shower Edge

I was a kid when I stood at the edge of a summer rain shower. Walking from the Harris Jr grocery store where I got a cherry Coke Slurpee and Sugar Babies, I was a block from my DeLowe Dr home when a sudden rain soaked me, making me sprint for home, chocolate candy spilling.

And suddenly I was back in the sun, and I stopped in confusion. Spinning in my wet Keds, the boundary of the rain was three feet from me, literally stopping right at the Elinwood Dr curb like a magician's curtain.

Astounded, I walked back to the rain, and from my dry place, stuck my right hand back into the storm. As a kid I just assumed that if it was raining on me, it was raining everywhere. But, no!

My Scouting memories

As I dipped the oar into the murky, green water, I was shocked to spot a section of submerged barbed wire fence. Our scout leader already warned us not to swim in the man-made lake because it wasn't deep and there were parts of fence that had snared boy scouts of Olde and drowned them.

My youth in scouts yielded scary stories like that; every area we camped in had eerie, creepy stories and *every* camp claimed to be the actual location of Doc Snyder, who died, leaving the "waterheads" in his secluded facility free to wander the woods and kill hapless fat scouts like me. None of us knew what waterheads were, but they sounded scary in the stories.

My church, East Point First Methodist, sponsored the troop and I also went to camp with the YMCA on Campbelton Rd across from the Krystal, and every Y camp claimed to be the real home of Doc Snyder's murderous waterheads, too.

Those stories, told over popping, smoky campfires, thrilled me almost as much as did the wienies we roasted there, impailed on oscillating sticks sharpened with our official BSA knives.

The submerged barbed wire fence let me live, and when our canoe reached the far shore, a scout from another troop rushed over, shouting: "Go back, you sissies! Waterheads are attacking our camp!"

My Stepmother Kept Grease Jar On Her Stove

My first stepmother had a metal jar. She kept it next to the stove and drained the black iron skillet into it after frying bacon. When she needed grease for cooking, she'd take it from this container. I've been told popcorn cooked in this kind of grease doesn't need butter for flavor.

Poe-lease vs Police

I knocked on the housing project door hard, the way we cops do.

Almost immediately, someone shouted through the door: "Who's there?"

It was 1980 and I was an APD investigator following up on a robbery report. "Police officer," I answered.

"Who?" I'd been attending classes at GSU and had been selling my writing to Creative Loafing, Atlanta magazine, and others, and I felt it important to be articulate. "Police officer," I repeated.

"WHO?"

My girlfriend typed her doctoral dissertation (French Lit) on my typewriter, in our East Point home, that I used to write about ghosts and true crime. I needed to act like A Writer.

"WHO?!"

With a sigh, I said "Poe-lease!" The resident, opening his door, muttered "Why didn't ya *say* so!"

Pretty Christmas light

Christmas. Light. It was maybe 1966, making me 10, in our house on DeLowe Dr, near the woods where a creek meandered, temporarily frozen.

I'd gotten out of bed to go to the bathroom. I stopped in the small hallway. Lights from the

Christmas tree in the next room illuminated the black, rotary phone on its stand; a strand of lights blinked like a lighthouse, making me feel like a ship at sea, fearful of encountering a dangerous reef.

My father and first stepmother – a big, angry woman wearing a twitchy, Christmas smile – watched Star Trek.

The lights on the tree were so beautiful: reds, frog-greens, ice-cream-oranges. On Christmas morning, light reflecting from a yard of white snow, where I could also see the plastic icicles, one melted a little from being too close to a hot light; and angel-hair, glistening and made of spun glass strands that cut your fingers when you tossed it on the tree. My father filmed the opening of gifts, holding an 8mm movie camera in his left hand while illuminating us with a hand-held metal spotlight so powerful it burned oxygen from the room, and was probably used in the war to spot Nazi bombers in the London clouds. One of my step-sisters got a Polaroid Swinger and insisted we take pictures of her; the photos had to be painted with lacquer to keep them from fading. I got a cheap Instamatic camera whose light cube flashed so bright it melted the cube, reeking of burnt plastic.

In a few days, the strands of light, icicles, and angel-hair would be boxed and returned to the frigid, dark attic. Light reveals so much, and pretty Christmas lights can conceal so much.

Reporter Still In High School

When the teacher frowned and rushed to me, I reached into my pocket and pulled it out.

I had to go an extra quarter to graduate Headland High School, but I had been hired as a reporter for the *Atlanta Suburban Reporter* in East Point. At the end of my second class, I reported to the newspaper office on Main St. I forget what the story was, but there was a press conference being held at Briarcliff HS; all students were supposed to be in class.

When the teacher saw me, she assumed I was a disobeying student and rushed to me hissing: "*All students are supposed to be in class!*" Without a word I pulled my press pass ID from my pocket. When she saw it, she stopped with an embarrassed look. "Sorry, sir," she blurted and I continued to the press conference, a bit too smugly.

Rescue Trip, I cannot believe dogs don't have a soul

Rescue Trip was a bait dog as a pup and the fighter dogs mauled him so bad we had to amputate a leg; I'm one of the only men he now let's near him. His troubled life troubles my heart.

I go to the kennel every week to play with him; he looks so deeply into my eyes that I cannot believe dogs don't have a soul; his kisses are a gift from God.

School Film You Are There

It was probably the 8th grade. The film projector made a clattering noise and an announcer intoned: "Lee is about to surrender to Grant at Appomattox court house. AND YOU ARE THERE!"

What followed was a Walter Cronkite show where they acted as if CBS was covering this historic event for the nightly news. I remember another one about the death of Socrates and the battle for the Alamo. I was totally enthralled.

Seeing Charles Chips brings back memories....

After a roast beef lunch at Cracker Barrel I spotted a bag of Charles Chips in their store and it opened memories: when I was a kid, one of our neighbors had Charles Chips in a tin barrel delivered to their door. Me and other kids gathered and watched this novelty.

Charles Chips was special, When I tasted some, at our neighbor's, I convinced myself they were better'n what my family bought at Harris Jr's.

So I snatched the bag off the Cracker Barrel shelf and looked forward to snacking on it while watching cable that evening. When I ripped the bag open, I half-expected unicorns to fly out as I dug in. It was ok, but I won't stop buying Lays.

Six Flags press conference luncheon

Free chicken cordon bleu!
When I was an *Atlanta Suburban Reporter* writer / cartoonist, I covered boring city council meetings and local gardeners who'd grown a rutabaga that, she thought, resembled John Wayne.

One day I received a letter addressed to me from Ken Baldowski, head of 6 Flags Over Georgia's PR. I was a friend of the Baldowski family. Kenny's dad, famous *Atlanta Constitution* political cartoonist "Baldy", Clifford Baldowski Sr, had recommended me for employment to the ASR's publisher. Kenny's brother, Bill Baldowski, was my friendly rival, a reporter for the *Neighbor* newspapers. Ken sent a letter inviting me to a press conference announcing a new 6 Flags ride around 1975. Chicken cordon bleu would be served to us reporters.

About 30 of us in news media attended hungrily and caterers sat us at long tables covered by white tablecloths. Clutching a fork in each hand, I happily watched the food wagon approach, caterers quickly plucking down a little saucer. By little I mean tiny – I was a big southside boy used to chomping down at places like Johnny Reb's and the Smorgasbord, but when I decided to ask for another little tray, the succulent-smelling wagon had moved down the table.

After the very upswing presentation, the adorable PR lady invited us into the park for a free rampage and we journalists galloped in a stampede into 6 Flags. I was on the clock, but I felt like I was playing hooky. The log flume, the sky buckets, the haunted house. But my first stop was the food court for a cheeseburger and fries.

Starting to understand words

I recall being tucked under the covers, 4 or 5 years old, my father sitting on the side of the bed, a silhouette with the ceiling light forming a yellow halo. When we are growing we learn words by imitating their sounds without fully understanding their meaning.

"Now say your prayers and go to sleep," he said, as he did every night, and I started reciting the well-known child's bedtime prayer. I was shocked and frightened when I realized I was saying, "If I should – *die* – before I wake"! My mother had only recently died and the whole Life thing was like an angel of death squatting on my heaving chest.

In Conley Hills I learned to spell "train" and was amazed that – all of a sudden – the word "train" was everywhere I looked! Now that I'd learned to read it.

I was afraid of people living in Hapeville because, for years, I thought it was "Hateville".

During service at East Point First Methodist Church, I started viewing the adults suspiciously because they were openly praying "Our Farther who *aren't* in heaven." When I learned the archaic word "art" I began trusting the adult congregation again.

Even now, if someone asks directions to the public "bathroom", I shake my head and say: "You won't find any baths around here!"

Street thug joust

I had to explain to my rookie why I just walked right into that thug as we got out of my squad car.

"There's a code on The Street," I said as we resumed walking the sidewalk of The Strip on Peachtree St in 1979. I was born and raised in East Point; I'd driven through these streets a lot, but now, as a cop, I experienced a lifestyle I'd never known.

"That was a test. A street thug will walk toward a cop, acting like he doesn't see you, and if you politely step aside, you just lost the joust, you're a punk, unworthy of respect on the street."

My rookie's child-like face was dubious.

"If a cop is ever stupid enough to have sex with a hooker on his beat, or take a bribe from the pusher on the corner, he's lost all respect on these streets. A cop has to be good, and fair, or he may as well put in for a transfer to a desk job."

The rookie averted my eyes. He'll learn. Or else.

Tattoos Jiggle Like Annoying GIFs

The corpulent woman at the table next to me was shoveling her food so fast it made her tattoos jiggle like those annoying gifs on Twitter.

Think I see fish eyes in bath drain as kid

When I was about 4 I looked into the bathtub drain and noticed water drops forming silver globs as they passed through. Having been told the drain led to the ocean, I thought the silver globules were fish eyes, having swum up the pipe from the sea, and they were spying me as full of amazement as I was from spying them.

Tree Cutter In Thunder Storm

The tree cutter was a tough country guy. My neighbor hired him to take down a tree that was just a few feet from where I sat in my house, hearing my dogs bark angrily at the sound outside of saws and a wood-chipper.

He lopped off limbs at the top of the tall tree, even as black clouds moved in. As the rain and wind pelted him, he kept cutting. He stayed high up in the tree with the power saw until the thunder and lightning was directly over his head and finally shimmied down, cupping a cigarette as he stood, waiting for the storm to past so he could finish the job as he'd promised.

Trying to save little Leon in the projects

Yes, when I was an APD detective assigned to the Housing Authority, most housing projects were The Bad Lands, but it was also a classroom where little kids play Cops-N-Robbers. And the Cops were the bad guys.

Leon was little for his age – 8. All the kids ran the University Homes grounds unsupervised, and most avoided the mini-precinct next to it ("pigs") in West End, but not little Leon.

I was there at a desk in the summer of '97, talking on the phone, and he nestled next to me, interested in the cartoon doodles I drew.

"You interested in art, Leon?" I asked and he nodded, snot dribbling from his nose. Little kids, even in the mean projects, looked up to cops – until they are poisoned by the thugs who make that turf The Bad Lands. If I could convince some kid like Leon that we are really the good guys, some day he may be tempted to hurt a cop, and he might think back to me and decide we aren't his enemy.

Next time I saw him I gave him crayons and a coloring book and taught him to draw the outline, and then fill it in, the way my dad taught me. Leon was thrilled.

Days later I was back at the mini-precinct and I asked the uniform sarge how little Leon was doing. "He's banned from the precinct. Caught him stealing." The Bad Lands.

Turning on furnace first time in Fall

That hideous smell. Finally giving in to the chilly temps of Fall and turning on the furnace. It means saying goodbye to summer: grilling out; swimming; tee shirts and shorts! Sweating just a few days ago, now vigorously rubbing all your goose bumps. I – reluctantly – flip the on switch........ AAAARGH! That hideous smell!

Under Roswell Rd Bridge Rafting the Chattahoochee

I often rafted the Chattahoochee with friends, great fun! Under the roads was a strange interlude, out of the summer sun, hearing the constant banging echoes of traffic above you as your raft bobbed in the dark water.

Walk to Headland, radio in my pocket

I remember wearing a heavy jacket as I walked to Headland in the morning light. In the jacket pocket was a transistor radio.

I still recall the cold, the heavy jacket, seeing the school room lights burning in the gloom as I approach. And I remember these songs playing from my pocket. *Fire and Rain. Long Cool Woman In a Black Dress. Gimme Shelter. Sunshine* by Jonathan Edwards.....I reached out and grabbed the cold metal handle and pulled open the door and entered the round cafeteria, happily smelling doughnuts and strong coffee cooking, as my AM signal suddenly dropped off.

What My Dogs Hear Outside

When my dogs run to my back door and bark like maniacs, I know why.

They can hear a salamander serenade out in the yard. Grasshoppers making blades of grass vibrate like discordant gazoos. Chipmunks chewing acorns, sounding like nacho cheese-flavored Doritoes. The pickaxes of moles striking rocks as they tunnel!

"Go get 'em, girls!"

Work at gas station at 16

Once upon a time, no kidding, a car rolled over a black rubber hose that snaked across all gas stations – *Ding! Ding!* – and an attendant ran out and pumped your gas.

In 1972 I was 16 and was a part-time attendant at the Chevron at the corner of Headland and DeLowe, while I attended Headland HS.

Across the street was Fogg's Shell, a true East Point landmark. On the other corner was the Gulf station where a cheerful man called "Fats" worked; he was always smiling, his gold tooth gleaming, and laughing and I figured if a car ran over his toe he'd double over – laughing!

I would scurry out, ask the driver "How much?" and I would pump their gas and squeegee their windows and check their oil.

One afternoon I told a driver "You're a quart low!" and he said "Add a quart, son!" Which I did, only, to my horror, realizing I put in transmission fluid instead of oil.

Running to Jim, the owner, to confess, he threw his arms up and exclaimed: "He'll probably sue me! I'll lose my station! My house!"

He scurried to Mike the mechanic and blurted "What can we do?"

Mike chuckled, like Fats might do, and said "Transmission fluid is just more refined than oil. It's probably better for the engine than regular oil."

I – and Jim – were greatly relieved.

I collected $6.20 and the driver rode over the black hose – *Ding! Ding!* – heading to Harris Jr for a cold Slushee.

The big screen goes dark and the lights in that theater of my subconscious come on, hurting my eyes.

Seems there are no more of my memories. And if that old wives' tale is true, about why our life flashes before our eyes when it does, I have a favor to ask. If you come across a scared dog, who has no home or family of its own, please Rescue it and offer it Lap Therapy. It might be me, reincarnated.

My books are available at Amazon.com. Put this link in to your browser:

http://amzn.to/2ia1DMT .

A Christmas For Healing. I was put on Earth to write this story. This is its fourth printing.
Emmett Nagel is a cop wounded in the line of duty. His smashed body has turned his soul dark and cold. Buoyed by his loving wife, Emmett is about to learn that you can't help yourself without first trying to help others.

Rescue Dog Rescue Me 2   Dog is God spelled backward.

Steve Cartwright, a retired cop and former newspaper writer, turned his love for dogs into his passion for dog Rescue. Helping those saved from death row was good for this long-time Rescuer's soul.

Also meet Dog Therapist Barry, so attuned to dogs' Wolf Nature he seemed like a shaman mystic.

Kenna, a saver of abused dogs, often saw them touched by such blessings they could only be bestowed by God.

They work with dogs who need help: Callie started out a trouble-maker but became a brave service dog for a wounded Marine.

Ava snapped at certain people, but time – and love – turned her into a sweet companion.

Jack -- what, or who, made this black lab so terrified? Could Jack be saved? And dozens of other Rescue dogs and their tragic, sweet stories that every dog-lover will thrill to. 168 photos.

Rescue Dog Rescue Me   A veteran dog Rescuer shows you how his way of helping homeless dogs has evolved after he let his first Rescue out of the cage and they, almost all, jumped into his lap. And he learned more: Shelter Syndrome. Lap Therapy. Foster Fail. Volunteers help dogs by loving them, playing with them. The Rescuer is often the first to ever give love to these abused dogs.158 photos.

I Dream Of Oddkins   A new book of surreal cartoons. In it a familiar-looking psychology guy explains about how the Id is like a dark basement in our subconscious. In that basement, things called Oddkins hide, casting our dreams & nightmares on a spinning wheel of magick.

Dark Tales From Gents' Pens (Annie Acorn's Dark Tales Book 1)

Where can you find all the suspense, thrills, blood, and gore that reflect the dark underbelly of our world? Where do murder and voodoo curses stand alongside innocents and little children? Where do the kinder, gentler things disappear? Within the tightly crafted stories gathered for your enjoyment by Annie Acorn into Dark Tales From Gents' Pens!

With their skillfully woven tales, the founding members of From Gents' Pens, a cooperative of award-winning contemporary male writers, have forged a unique collection of stories that are sure to please those who enjoy a tingle running up and down their spines, as they face the monsters who no longer linger beneath their beds.

Contains: